KT-151-129

WORLD CUP 2003

*The Official Account
of England's World Cup
Triumph*

Also by Team England Rugby

Grand Slam Champions

WORLD CUP 2003

*The Official Account
of England's World Cup
Triumph*

TEAM ENGLAND RUGBY

ORION

Copyright © 2003 Team England Rugby

Fifth impression 2003

The right of Team England Rugby to be identified as the author
of this work has been asserted by them in accordance with
the Copyright, Designs and Patents Act 1988

All rights reserved. No part of this publication may be
reproduced, stored in a retrieval system, or transmitted
in any form or by any means, electronic, mechanical,
photocopying, recording or otherwise without the prior
permission of the copyright owner

First published in Great Britain in 2003 by Orion
an imprint of Orion Books Ltd
Orion House, 5 Upper St Martin's Lane, London WC2H 9EA

A CIP catalogue record for this book is available
from the British Library

ISBN 0 75286 048 8

Printed and bound by
Butler & Tanner Ltd, Frome and London

Contents

Acknowledgements

Team England Rugby would like to thank Ian Stafford, Richard Prescott and Dee McIntosh at the RFU, Robert Kirby and Maria Dawson at PFD, Freddie Nuttall, Annabel Taylor and Sarah Bentley at CSS-Stellar, Malcolm Edwards, Ian Preece, Richard Hussey, Paul Hussey, Helen Ewing and Nick May at Orion, Philip Parr, Jonathan Fordham, Ros Ellis, and Getty Images, particularly Neil Loft, Brendan Kemp and Paul Ashman.

Jason Leonard

Ben Cohen

Ben Kay

Martin Johnson

Joe Worsley

Dan Luger

Paul Grayson

Danny Grewcock

Kyran Bracken

Mike Tindall

Matt Dawson

Stuart Abbott

Lawrence Dallaglio

Martin Corry

Jonny Wilkinson

Iain Balshaw

Neil Back

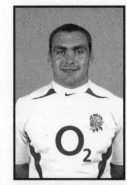

Trevor Woodman

Lewis Moody

Julian White

Dorian West

Mark Regan

Andy Gomarsall

Will Greenwood

Josh Lewsey

Phil Vickery

Steve Thompson

Richard Hill

Jason Robinson

Mike Catt

Simon Shaw

Clive Woodward

Rugby World Cup England Squad 2003

Introduction

It's difficult to say exactly when England's long campaign to win the Rugby World Cup began. Some would argue you should go back to the autumn of 1997, when Clive Woodward took the reins and launched an ambitious and concerted effort to transform England into the best side in the world. Others may say it started when Martin Johnson became captain in the summer of 1999. Certainly, from 1997 onwards, the English international test squad has been on a sharp upward curve. First came their domination of the Five/Six Nations. However, while titles were won, the Grand Slam repeatedly eluded them. Were these desperate setbacks or lessons from which the team could learn and grow? It would now seem to be the latter.

The Grand Slam finally came in the spring of 2003, and it set up England for a memorable summer tour Down Under. They would win a test for only the second time ever in New Zealand, and then achieve a *first* victory against Australia, in Australia, just one week later. Coming less than a year after 2002's home victories against the two Antipodean sides and South Africa, England were justifiably now ranked the number-one team in the world. But rankings meant nothing to Clive Woodward, Martin Johnson, or anyone else in the England camp. Only the world champions could truly say they were the best team in the world, and they were Australia.

If this England side had learned some harsh lessons in the Six Nations, the World Cup had provided a painful one, too. For the management and many of the senior players, losing to South Africa in the 1999 quarter-final had been a crushing blow that had left the team shell-shocked. Yet it had also made them determined to bounce back, bigger, stronger, faster and better than ever. From virtually the moment the final whistle had blown in Paris, England's eyes had turned to Australia, 2003.

Officially, England's World Cup campaign really began with three warm-up test matches in the late summer of 2003. The point of these was not so much to stretch the team's streak of test wins, but to see who would come through in the face of stiff opposition to make Clive Woodward's final World Cup squad of thirty. Four years previously, by his own admission, the head coach had made a mistake by not trusting his fringe players to do a job at the World Cup. This time around, he was determined to make full use of every one of his thirty men. Fortunately, with the strength in depth of English rugby, Woodward was well aware that every member of the squad would be a player of the highest quality. For some, of course, there was heart-break when they failed to make it on to the plane Down Under. For others, pure joy, which could only have been heightened by the fact that they were going to Australia with a great chance of lifting the trophy.

But being favourites is one thing. Winning is another. And England were not short of competition. New Zealand had cut a swath through the Tri Nations tournament earlier in the year and looked as formidable as ever. One of the teams they had trounced, South Africa, had picked a young but exciting squad and seemed to be on the way up. Ireland and France were clearly dangerous, while there were hints that something was stirring in the Welsh valleys, too.

Then there was Australia. Roundly criticised Down Under for a series of disappointing results, the Wallabies had a habit of getting it right when it really mattered. As defending champions, playing in front of home crowds, they could not be written off.

And so began seven weeks of drama and theatre, passion, power, skill, speed and entertainment. The minnows had their moments in the sun, but when it came down to the business end of the tournament, the traditional heavyweights squared up to slug it out. There were mutterings back home that England were struggling. Stretched by South Africa, behind for most of the game against Samoa, and at half-time against a rejuvenated Wales in the quarter-final, had they perhaps peaked before the competition had even begun? The answer, as the French discovered in the semi-final, was an emphatic 'No'. The French, along with New Zealand, had lit up the tournament in the group stages with dashing rugby. But England and fellow finalists Australia proved that, in a World Cup tournament, early form ultimately counts for nothing.

Thus the stage was set for the World Cup Final: the hosts and defending champions against the number-one team in the world, and the old rivals to boot. On paper it looked good, but the match itself would eclipse anything anyone could have imagined. It would go down as the greatest game of rugby ever, with the most dramatic and memorable of conclusions. England, led by the incomparable Martin Johnson, and propelled by the magic of Jonny Wilkinson, would win the day and the World Cup. It would be the end of an incredible journey.

This is the story of that journey, often told in the players' own words. It is the story of how a group of men stuck together through thick and thin, failure and success, with a single aim in mind. It is the story of how new names have become etched in the national sporting psyche. And it is the story of how one rainy, glorious night in Sydney will be relived for decades to come. English sport, *British* sport, had been deprived of success for far too long. For the England rugby team, it was payback time. They duly delivered.

Chapter 1

WALES   9–43   ENGLAND

Saturday 23 August
at the Millennium Stadium, Cardiff

Wales: R. Williams, M. Jones, Taylor, Parker, Gareth Thomas, S. Jones (Captain), Cooper, I. Thomas, McBryde (G. Williams, 61), Jenkins (A. Jones, 71), Sidoli, Wyatt (J. Thomas, 62), Charvis, M. Williams, D. Jones (Gavin Thomas, 71)

Pens: S. Jones 3

England: Scarborough, Simpson-Daniel, Noon, Abbott, Luger (Smith, 57), King (Walder, 72), Gomarsall, Leonard (Captain), Regan (West, 38), White (Green, 72), Grewcock, Shaw, Corry, Moody (Sanderson, 62), Worsley

Tries: Moody, Luger, Worsley, Abbott, West
Cons: King 2, Walder
Pens: King 3
Drop Goal: King

Referee: P. Deluca (Argentina)

Attendance: 60,000

Exactly one month after England's stunning win over Australia in Melbourne, the preliminary World Cup squad of forty-three players returned to duty at the Pennyhill Park Hotel in Bagshot, the official team base, where they would be living for the best part of ten weeks.

Head coach Clive Woodward had announced his squad the week before. After three summer tests against Wales in Cardiff and France both away and at home, the forty-three would be whittled down to a final thirty, who would have the responsibility of representing England, by now the clear favourites, in the World Cup.

'This squad of players is based on the fact that everyone is fit to play in the three World Cup preparation games,' said Woodward. 'There are still a couple of players who have an outside chance of making the [final] squad and I will be monitoring them through their clubs. In total there are fifty names that are being submitted to the World Cup for accreditation purposes.'

From the moment when Martin Johnson and his men arrived in Bagshot all eyes were finally firmly focused on the World Cup. The jobs of the previous season – securing the Grand Slam and winning triumphantly in the Southern Hemisphere – had been done, and the team was refreshed after a much-needed holiday, though their choices in that respect were sometimes a little out of the ordinary. Josh Lewsey had spent a fortnight white-water rafting and then working on a cattle ranch in true *City Slickers* style. 'I wore a Stetson, boots, chaps, the lot,' the England full-back said. 'I looked like John Wayne. It was a great chance for me to get away from it all for a while, and to throw myself into a few challenges. I was rounding up cattle, branding, and doing a lot of riding.' Now, however, the fun would have to stop.

Over the course of the next four weeks Clive Woodward and his world-class team of specialist coaches would be fine-tuning their impressive collection of players, making assessments and ensuring that England's preparation for the tournament was spot on.

The first of England's three warm-up internationals would be against a struggling Wales in Cardiff, but in the month up to then the rugby spotlight would be off the Grand Slam champions, for once. Followers of the game were focused on the Tri Nations series, which saw New Zealand crowned as champions after demolishing both Australia and South Africa away with record scores, and then defeating them both at home in closer contests. The Wallabies and Springboks beat each other on their own turf, although the fixture in Brisbane was marred by allegations against South Africa of foul play, specifically biting. Clive Woodward and Wallaby coach Eddie Jones joined forces to condemn the Springboks, which added even more spice to the forthcoming World Cup group game between England and South Africa in October. 'I can't disagree with Eddie too much,' said Woodward after Jones had branded South Africa 'a disgrace' . Although, perhaps optimistically, he continued, 'I don't think what you're seeing now will have any bearing on the World Cup.'

Down Under, everyone was talking up the English, especially the victorious All Blacks. 'England are still the team to beat,' insisted their flying wing, Joe Rokocoko, moments after beating Australia to claim both the Bledisloe Cup and Tri Nations. Former All Black coach John Hart weighed in, too. 'My heart says New Zealand but my head says England,' he declared. 'Why? Because to win the World Cup you need a big forward pack, an excellent goal-kicker and backs capable of utilising forward dominance. England have got all that.'

Back home in the Surrey countryside, those senior players who missed out on the June party through injury were intent on making up for lost ground. At least some of them knew that time was fast running out. For Charlie Hodgson, out since injuring his left cruciate knee ligament against Italy

> 'My heart says New Zealand but my head says England.'
>
> *JOHN HART*

during the Six Nations, time seemed to have run out already. 'The latest medical reports we have suggest Charlie won't be playing any rugby before 8 September,' reported Woodward. 'I don't think Charlie will make it.'

Hodgson himself tried to be positive: 'I'm extremely disappointed to miss out but I'm young and have plenty of time in the future to make amends,' he said. 'I've had a bit of time to come to terms with it and I'll be a better player and a stronger person for the experience.'

Woodward also rated Bath's Mike Catt as doubtful, although he had not entirely given up on the utility back who had been fighting a chronic hamstring problem. The England management would watch the experienced international in the Middlesex Sevens and in a club game the following day. Also playing in the Sevens would be Leicester flanker Lewis Moody, who was recovering from a shoulder operation. Meanwhile, both Austin Healey and Julian White declared themselves ready to play after knee operations. For Moody, even being in the frame again was a triumph after an injury-plagued six months during which England seemed to have done perfectly well without him. 'If the team perform superbly, as England have, then you know it's going to be twenty times harder to get back in, but you're a very lucky man if you get through a whole career in rugby without at least one serious injury.

'Most of the England boys have been there and know how you are feeling

> **'Players of world renown have been training like seventeen-year-old apprentices trying to break into the first team.'**
>
> *MATT DAWSON*

and have felt on the periphery of things. Lawrence Dallaglio had a shocking knee injury and had to sit out a season but has come back stronger and better than ever. If I started to fret a bit in the summer I just stood back for five minutes and reminded myself how strongly Lawrence eventually came back. It's also been nice to get a few text messages from Clive Woodward when England were touring, just asking how things were coming on.'

Another player back in the fold was Danny Grewcock, omitted from the June tour after he was sent off for punching Lawrence Dallaglio during the Parker Pen Challenge Cup Final. He spent the summer in deep contemplation on a Croatian island. 'I am determined to keep my nose clean from now on,' he insisted. 'I won't be getting into any more trouble. Will power, amazing will power. That's how I'll do it. I'm just pleased to be back in the squad with a chance of going to the World Cup. Second row has always been an incredibly competitive area, so I guess one of maybe five of us will be disappointed when the final squad is announced.'

Already the thought of that final selection was preying on the players' minds, even the well established, such as Matt Dawson. 'Forty-three into thirty won't go,' he said. 'Thirteen top-quality, super-fit rugby players will miss out, despite working themselves to a standstill this summer. The upcoming games are big enough as it is before the added pressure of trying to win your World Cup berth.

'That's probably why I've never seen such enthusiasm, and the work-rate has been awesome. Nobody has spared themselves or left anything in the tank. It has been flat out from day one and totally inspiring to train in such an environment. Players of world renown have been training like seventeen-year-old apprentices trying to break into the first team.'

For Woodward, of course, the three warm-up games were scheduled to provide him with the information he needed to judge which of his fringe players would be good enough to make the trip Down Under. Although he already knew his strongest fifteen, and just about his strongest twenty-two, for that matter, those eight extra berths were up for grabs. So, unlike four years previously, when some players had remained on the sidelines in the build-up to the World Cup, Woodward was determined to give everyone at least one chance at some point in the three games.

'I am very happy to put any combination of fifteen from that forty-three on the field in England shirts against any team in the world,' he declared on the eve of deciding who would face the Welsh at the Millennium Stadium. 'A lesson from 1999 was that we weren't confident enough to use our squad fully. Since then, however, we have been able to improve our strength in depth immeasurably.

'Looking back, we hadn't tested ourselves enough mentally, put ourselves on the line enough, in the build-up four years ago. That had to change. I want tests and challenges. It's in our interest to see everybody for the full duration over the next three warm-up tests. That will be part of the data we need for selection. Barring injuries, I won't be looking to make any changes at all.'

Twenty-four hours later Woodward stuck to his guns by naming a twenty-two full of interesting choices. It was a radically different side to the England that had defeated Australia in Melbourne, the last time the team had played an international. Although the venerable Jason Leonard would be leading the side for only the second time in his thirteen-year international career, the rest of the big hitters were kept on the sidelines. The reason for this was simple enough: the likes of Martin Johnson, Jonny Wilkinson, Lawrence Dallaglio and the other Grand Slam heroes knew that they would be on the plane. The likes of Martin Corry, Stuart Abbott, Jamie Noon and others certainly did not. Wasps centre Abbott and the Leeds full-back Dan Scarborough were given their first caps, while Lewis Moody and Julian White, both out of action through injury since February, were given the chance to remind everyone of their international pedigree. Danny Grewcock, who would have been pushing Ben Kay hard for the second slot alongside Johnson in the second row in the summer had he not been suspended, was also back in the team, while the Wasps fly-half, Alex King, would be looking not only to cement his place as Wilkinson's understudy but to bring out the best in the tyro centre pairing of Noon and Abbott.

'This is not an England second team,' Woodward said emphatically. 'There are players coming back from injury and suspension as well as those that are pushing very, very hard for first-team places. It's a full-on international with caps awarded. Winning the game is obviously very important for England, but it's equally important to make sure that I get it right when I pick the final thirty on 8 September. There's a lot of pressure on this team and there's a lot at stake for them as individuals.'

The only other time Leonard had captained his country – against Argentina in 1996 – he scored his sole international try. Would he be looking for his second this time around? 'I'm not the man people rush out to put a tenner on to score the first try in a match,' he said. 'It will be business as usual in that respect.'

And business as usual in every other respect, too, for the man set to win his 104th cap, just seven behind French centre Philippe Sella's world record.

Leonard's total, of course, does not include a further six caps won playing for the Lions. In being named captain, Leonard would be leading out his men in Cardiff at the age of thirty-five, equalling the achievement of the great All Black Colin Meads as the oldest international skipper.

Leonard's attention was on more pressing concerns than the record-books, though. He knew that he was by no means a certainty to take his chance in a fourth successive World Cup, a fact confirmed by Woodward. 'I've never seen Jason in better shape,' admitted the head coach. 'He's done a great job already, but he's got to play very well to put pressure on the other props. I haven't decided whether we will take four or five to the World Cup.'

Leonard accepted this phlegmatically. 'I see my role as helping as many people as I can,' he said, 'making sure they cope with the pressure and put in a performance at the same time. I have no idea how many props will go to the World Cup. It's a case of putting your name on the list, and hoping it will be nearer the top than the bottom. I feel very good at the moment and I'm enjoying being part of the best-prepared England squad I've ever been involved with.'

'I feel very good at the moment and am enjoying being part of the best-prepared England squad I've ever been involved with.'

JASON LEONARD

The day after naming his team, Woodward sent out a clear message to his men that he expected not only best form, but best behaviour. 'The players are under no illusions that if we think they can't cope with that sort of thing then they will not go to the World Cup,' he reiterated. 'Self-discipline is an area of massive importance to us. That's not to say that we play like angels, because it's important that we're on the edge. But we can't afford to lose a game because we had a guy in the sin bin or sent off.'

Grewcock had already made the pledge that his bad-boy days were behind him. Now it was the turn of Julian White, who had been forced to sit out the triumphant back-to-back test victories over the big three from the Southern Hemisphere the previous autumn after receiving a ten-week ban for punching. 'I've let myself down in the past and I'm determined not to go down that road again,' promised the thirty-year-old prop. 'Clive has shown faith in me and it's up to me to repay that. If I'm stupid enough to do something, then it will be on my own head.'

It was clear that the game against the Welsh, billed as just a World Cup warm-up friendly in the press, was much more than that for all of the players who would be taking the field. For Dan Luger, one of the most lethal finishers in the game, it was a chance to confirm his return to the big time now that, hopefully, the injuries that had blighted his career were behind him. Having agreed to leave Harlequins for the south of France and Perpignan, the Heineken Cup runners-up, Luger was hoping he would not be called into action by the French club until after the World Cup. 'This has been my first pre-season for some time because of my various injuries, and it does take a while to get right back into everything,' he said. 'I felt I was lucky to be on the bench for the last couple of Six Nations matches. Having had to battle back from my serious knee injury, that was a real bonus, especially after the shock of losing my good friend Nick Duncombe as well earlier in the year. I think that has affected my outlook a great deal. I remember telling Nick that he should have bought a flat instead of a flash car, but now I realise that as he loved his car so much he did the right thing. I'm intent on enjoying myself a great deal more from now on and, now that I'm feeling strong and fit again, I'm ready to take what chances come my way.' These words would prove to be prophetic a few days later.

Alex King was keen to seize his big opportunity. Six years after ruling himself out of England's team in their first match under Clive Woodward, the Wasps stand-off would be wearing the England number-ten jersey for the first time in his fifth cap, but his first start. 'I'm sure there will be tears in my mum's eyes,' he said when hearing of his selection. 'My whole family will be travelling down to Cardiff to see the match and, yes, it will be a special moment for me to run out in such a famous stadium against one of the major rugby nations as the England outside-half.

'Winning the Zurich Premiership with Wasps meant I could come into the squad with my head held high and the confidence is still there. Having been on the replacements' bench seventeen times, this is a dream come true for me.'

It's easy to understand his sentiments. The new England coach had plumped for King against Australia at Twickenham in November 1997, only for the player to withdraw forty-eight hours before kick-off rather than gamble on a troublesome knee. Instead of becoming Woodward's first fly-half, he would be the coach's ninth starter in the position, some sixty-five tests later.

'I pulled out because I would not have done myself justice,' King said. 'I thought that by playing I'd be letting the team down. If you don't play well, you might not get another chance. I obviously thought I'd get another opportunity because I was in the frame. Six years later, here I am.'

Back in 1997 the number-ten jersey had been up for grabs after the incumbent for the previous decade, Rob Andrew, had retired. Woodward had turned to Mike Catt when King dropped out, but within a few months Jonny Wilkinson's potential had become obvious to everyone. 'I might have played against Australia if I'd known,' joked King. 'I hadn't heard he was coming through.'

Two days before the test, Woodward named his seven substitutes. This was unusual as normally they are named on the Tuesday, together with the starting fifteen. The main point of interest here was the inclusion of Austin Healey, who had won, at least partially, his long battle for fitness after recurring knee trouble had eliminated him from first the Grand Slam and then the tour to Australasia. The only back of the modern era to have played test rugby in all seven positions behind the scrum, Healey's versatility was the reason why Woodward had given him every chance to make the World Cup squad. Despite this, the thirty-year-old Leicester Tiger, who had not represented his country for eighteen months, knew his chances were slim. 'I am probably a huge outsider to go to the World Cup because of the competition I'm up against and because I haven't played for so long,' he admitted. 'I'm training full-on all day. If that proves good enough to get me to the World Cup, fantastic. Being back in action at the England training camp, I realise how much the squad has moved on since my last match. The standards are higher than ever, the competition greater than ever. It's an incredibly difficult task, but if I don't make it, it won't be for any lack of hard work on my part.'

Wales, meanwhile, would be fielding eight of the team that had suffered a 9–26 Six Nations defeat in the same stadium the previous February. Of these players – Gareth Thomas, Rhys Williams, Mark Taylor, Gareth Cooper, Iestyn Thomas, Robert Sidoli, Martyn Williams and Dafydd James – only Gareth Thomas remained of the team that had played Ireland in Dublin the previous weekend and been trounced 35–12.

Wales also chose their eighth captain in three years, handing the job to Llanelli stand-off Stephen Jones. He succeeded Martyn Williams, even though the Cardiff flanker was included in the back row. Of the other six captains, Colin Charvis and Gareth Thomas retained their places in a team which also featured the return of New Zealand-born centre Sonny Parker. 'This is a huge match,' announced Stephen Jones. 'We are giving England the greatest respect.'

Such sentiments were echoed by Wales and Lions hooker Robin McBryde. 'Any side that England puts out will be strong,' he said. 'It should be a good challenge for us and it shouldn't take us long to knit together as a group.'

That proved to be more than a little over-optimistic. Come the match, Clive Woodward's England team, strong in personnel but still very much a second fifteen, handed out a brutal thrashing to the best side Wales could muster. It stretched England's record to fourteen straight wins and gave Woodward the kind of selection headache that all other coaches must envy.

Sporting no more than one or two possible starters from the first-choice fifteen, England notched up their biggest winning margin ever in Wales.

They scored five unanswered tries against a team they could well meet in the World Cup quarter-final. And, gratifyingly for all those involved in English rugby, England finally drew level with Wales in a series that has raged since 1881. Each side now has forty-nine wins; but England has won ten of the last eleven.

'Any side that England puts out will be strong.'

ROBIN McBRYDE

However, it was not an entirely satisfactory display by England. Although starting and finishing well, there were patchy spells, especially after the interval, when Alex King missed three consecutive kicks at goal. Even so, to record a 34-point win away in Cardiff in the height of summer during a conditioning programme was probably as good as Woodward and his management team could have expected. The performance of certain individuals also gave the head coach food for thought.

The win was founded on a superb display from the tight five, which proved so dominant that England enjoyed an embarrassment of territory and possession. No unit made better hay of this than the back row, where Lewis Moody and Joe Worsley were especially effective. Martin Corry, in his first full international since starting for the Lions back in 2001, also made a valuable contribution. Indeed, the Leicester war-horse lost over three kilos in the August sunshine. Andy Gomarsall, seemingly battling it out with Austin Healey for the third scrum-half's place in the final squad, also impressed to such an extent that Healey acknowledged he would hard pressed now to keep Gomarsall out of the final World Cup squad.

On the flip side, Dan Scarborough had not done himself justice, while King, in addition to his average kicking display, which saw a total of six attempts sail wide, failed to get his backs up to steam. The inexperienced centres Jamie Noon and Stuart Abbott, battling with Ollie Smith for a replacement centre berth, failed to produce any bite in the back line.

With so much at stake for England's reserve players, it was no surprise that they approached the game with gusto straight from the kick-off. Once the ball had been gathered, the first move went through ten phases and twenty-three pairs of hands before finally breaking down.

King had already missed once when Stephen Jones, against the run of play, nudged Wales ahead with an 11th-minute penalty. Four minutes later King steadied his nerves by equalising with a penalty, and on 18 minutes he gave England the lead with another.

Lewis Moody then announced his return to test rugby with a 24th-minute try. Simon Shaw's presence in the line-out meant that the Leicester flanker was given the perfect chance to bulldoze his way over the line, using Jason Leonard in the process as a gridiron-style blocker. 'He barged me out of the way,' complained a smiling Leonard later.

A further two penalties from Jones sandwiched a sweetly struck King drop goal, so the teams went in at half-time with England only seven points ahead in spite of their dominance. It was oddly reminiscent of the match in 1999's Five Nations when England had trounced Wales in the first half but had been only seven points ahead at the break. Then, of course, Wales had hit back in the second half to claim a dramatic late victory. But that was never going to happen this time.

Any lingering hopes of an unlikely Welsh victory were dashed when Dan Luger scored his 22nd try in only his 34th international after 55 minutes. Luger has Danny Grewcock to thank for his score. The Bath captain had launched into a thunderous run that opened up the Welsh defence before Corry and Noon, whose knock-on went unnoticed, got in on the act. Luger then had the chance to show his strength by reaching over the line to touch down. Grewcock's contribution typified the mood of the pack, who emerged after half-time with renewed vigour. As for Luger, he was delighted to be doing what he loves most. 'It was one of my least spectacular efforts for England,' he said, 'but they all count and I'm just very pleased to be scoring again. It doesn't matter if it's your first try or your twenty-second, they all provide a very happy feeling when you've touched down and you know the try will be given.'

King added the conversion and a subsequent penalty before a late onslaught by England produced three tries, and that record score. First Joe Worsley, who had scored in Cardiff during the Six Nations encounter earlier in the year, displayed his strength and fitness by brushing aside Colin Charvis as he crashed over from close range. 'Trying to break permanently into the England back row must be one of the hardest jobs in the world,' Worsley explained afterwards. 'All I can do is make some kind of a mark when I get a chance, which is why the try was so pleasing for me.'

Then Stuart Abbott marked his test debut with a try. The South African-born Wasp centre had already impressed during the game, as indeed he had during England's non-capped win over the New Zealand Maoris in Hamilton the previous June, but he then came on a sweet running angle to collect from substitute stand-off Dave Walder and touch down in the corner. 'The try was a fantastic feeling and finished off a great day in Cardiff,' twenty-five-year-old Abbott said later. 'I'm definitely going to keep my first England jersey, which is why I wouldn't swap it with any from the Welsh team. It's a treasured memory of a day I'll never forget.'

In the dying seconds hooker

> 'Trying to break permanently into the England back row must be one of the hardest jobs in the world.'
>
> *JOE WORSLEY*

Dorian West managed to bundle his considerable frame over the line after an unstoppable driving maul from the English forwards. His captain, Jason Leonard, light-heartedly claimed that he was thereby robbed of his second try for England: 'Dorian ripped the ball from my arms as we drove over from a line-out,' he said.

Afterwards the mood of the two head coaches could not have been more different. 'That was a poor, poor performance and a very painful experience,' said Wales's Kiwi boss Steve Hansen. 'England will be the best-prepared side in the World Cup and have got everything going for them.'

Woodward, by contrast, was understandably delighted. 'This win shows again what great strength we have and I'm going to have a very difficult decision when it comes to choosing the final squad,' he said. 'It was a pretty angry changing room at half-time because, although we created gaps, we weren't putting them away. But in the second half the sheer power of the team told. I'm sure the guys who didn't play would have taken note today.'

Andy Gomarsall spoke later of how he had spent the entire summer working his way through a list of improvements demanded by Woodward and his coaches in their end-of-season report. 'The major point was that I needed to be far more vocal in taking responsibility at the contact area,' he admitted. 'You get one hundred of those situations per game and sometimes I'd kept quiet when it came to giving instructions.

'Clive was honest with me. He said I'd get a full eighty minutes against Wales, and that was all the incentive I needed. This was a massive step for me and I keep thinking I'm saving my best for last. I just have to do my talking on the pitch.'

Another player to benefit from the game was Jason Leonard, who was singled out by Woodward for praise. 'Jason captained the team extraordinarily well,' said the head coach. Leonard, however, in typical fashion, was more concerned about his fellow forwards' efforts. 'When you've got that mixture of youth, power, pace and strength in the pack, it's going to be a hard game for anybody when you play well,' he insisted.

In 1999 the England starting fifteen for the first World Cup match of that year had just about picked itself, and those on the reserve list had been well down the pecking order. On the evidence of the match at the Millennium Stadium, however, virtually any of the forty-three players in the squad for 2003 could step up and do the job required of them on the greatest stage of all. Clive Woodward's problem, now just over a fortnight away, was to decide which thirty of the forty-three were the most deserving.

Chapter 2

FRANCE   17–16   ENGLAND

Saturday 31 August
at the Stade Vélodrome, Marseille

France: Brusque, Rougerie, Jauzion, Traille (Liebenberg, 54), Dominici, Michalak, Galthie (Captain), Crenca (Milloud, 67), Bru (Ibanez, 55), Marconnet, Pelous, Thion (Auradou, 65), Betsen (Tabacco, 57), Magne (Chabal, 76), Harinordoquy

Try: Brusque
Pens: Michalak 3
Drop Goal: Michalak

England: Balshaw (Walder, 54), Lewsey, Smith, Tindall (Gomarsall, 76), Cohen, Grayson, Healey, Rowntree (Leonard, 62), West (Captain; Thompson, 50), White, Borthwick (Shaw, 62), Grewcock, Corry, Moody, Sanderson

Try: Tindall
Con: Grayson
Pens: Grayson 3

Referee: M. Lawrence (South Africa)

Attendance: 60,000

The next stage in the delicate process of selection would take place just seven days later. With respect to Wales, facing France in Marseille would be a far more taxing proposition than taking on a beleaguered Welsh squad with little confidence.

Even fielding a full-strength, first-choice England fifteen would not guarantee anything against a team that can be the most destructive in the world, but, by using the game as a further opportunity to trial those on the fringes of the team, Woodward and co. would be facing a very thorough examination. In the end, it could be argued that honours were just about even after a fascinating international played in the balmy evening heat of France's second-largest city.

Earlier in the week, with England having packed hastily for the trip to Provence, Woodward had picked a team which was, once again, a faintly odd collection of players. For a start, England had a new captain, and an unlikely one at that. Dorian West, known throughout English rugby as 'Nobby', was appointed to lead his country six weeks short of his thirty-sixth birthday. In accepting the honour, the Leicester Tigers hooker became the tenth England captain under Clive Woodward and the oldest for almost half a century. (Another hooker, Eric Evans of Sale, had retired at thirty-six in 1958 after leading England to their first post-war Grand Slam.) Born in Wrexham, North Wales, West moved with his coal-mining family to the East Midlands, where he has been playing rugby ever since. His rise to eminence is one of the better examples of everything coming to he who waits.

After West resigned from the Leicestershire Constabulary, where he served in the Armed Response Unit, the former PC898 threw his lot into being a modern rugby player. In doing so, he managed to transform himself from the amateur culture of pies and pints to the new, demanding lifestyle of professionalism. But it's been a long time coming. Indeed, it took him the best part of ten years just to establish himself in the Leicester first team. 'You soon realised you couldn't mess about at weekends,' he recalled. 'You had to be training first thing Monday morning with a bunch of young lads who were mad keen to make an impression. It didn't take five minutes to appreciate you had to change your ways.'

A flanker at the Tigers in the late 1980s, he soon found himself losing out to a certain newcomer named Neil Back. Moving to Nottingham, he was persuaded by the ex-England and Leicester full-back Dusty Hare to switch positions to the front row. Then an outstanding performance for his new club in a cup tie persuaded his former team to take him back. 'All I remember is that Martin Johnson had me by the throat for most of the game and that nobody could get the ball off Dean Richards,' said West. 'Dusty Hare thought it might be an idea to switch me from my normal position in the back row to hooker so that I could get stuck into the ABC club [the Leicester front row, along with the rest of the team, wore lettered shirts then] and rough them up. It took me five years to learn the skills of scrummaging and throwing into the line-out to become a decent player.'

It was not until he had turned thirty that West finally won his first England cap, as a substitute, and another three years before he would play his first full international. Now, though, he appeared to be Australia-bound for the World Cup, together with first-choice England hooker Steve Thompson, and Mark Regan, with whom West would be battling for the reserve's place. 'I have done everything asked of me fitness-wise and answered every question,' West explained. 'I don't feel old. You get the odd creak but you learn to keep on top of your fitness.'

> 'I don't feel old. You get the odd creak but you learn to keep on top of your fitness.'
>
> *DORIAN WEST*

Certainly Clive Woodward had no qualms in choosing West as his latest leader. 'Dorian has captained England "A" very successfully and I think he is the obvious choice for the job,' the coach insisted.

West was realistic enough, however, not to get ideas above his station. Asked if he saw his appointment as a one-off or the start of something bigger, he laughed. 'You don't want to get too carried away with that sort of thinking,' he said. 'Besides, if you think too much about what you're going to do as a captain, then you're in trouble. You've got to be natural. It's about standing up and being counted, that's all.'

There were ten changes to the side which had thrashed Wales, as Woodward continued to sift through the World Cup contenders. There were call-ups for three men who had served England well when they had beaten Australia in Melbourne in June: Ben Cohen, Mike Tindall and Josh Lewsey, part of a backs line-up that included not one player who had turned out the previous weekend. Clearly, although the game was a trial, Woodward felt the need to give at least some of his big guns a run-out. By doing so, he hoped to counteract the obvious threat the French would pose, especially from their own powerful and devastatingly quick backs line.

One more peripheral player who was also given an opportunity was the injury-plagued Austin Healey. He was given a late, late chance to put himself back into the World Cup frame. Adept in so many positions, the Leicester Tiger was picked for where he had started and, indeed, where he had won his first England cap. Back at scrum-half, Healey knew he trailed Matt Dawson and Kyran Bracken, and was fighting it out with Andy Gomarsall for the third and final place in that position in the World Cup squad. He also realised that he had to produce an impressive display to nudge Gomarsall out of the reckoning after the Gloucester number nine's fine performance against the Welsh. 'I've been waiting for this chance for a long time,' said Healey, who had fifty caps to his name but had played only eleven games in 2002/3. 'It's funny, because I almost feel like a rookie again. It's all very invigorating.'

The American specialist who had saved Healey's career had earlier revealed the commitment that had propelled the Leicester utility back into last-minute contention. 'Austin has a work ethic like no athlete I have ever trained,' said Bill Knowles from his clinic in the mountains of Vermont. An expert in the non-surgical rehabilitation of smashed knees, Knowles had agreed to take Healey for the whole of June after the RFU had approached him. 'The first time I looked at him I saw a very motivated and very determined athlete,' he said. 'We worked on increasing the stability of the knee joint by increasing the neurological responses of the muscles. Austin's attitude was that he had nothing to lose. After one week he knew this was the right place to be and by the end of week two I knew he had a seventy per cent chance of making the World Cup. His focus on executing each knee movement correctly was outstanding.'

Healey's club colleague Ollie Smith was also hoping to impress after injury problems had hampered the twenty-one-year-old centre's season. Meanwhile, the venerable Paul Grayson was given a chance to claim the fly-half second spot behind Jonny Wilkinson, with both Alex King and Dave Walder also hoping to make the trip to the Southern Hemisphere. Although nothing had been decided at this stage, Woodward hinted strongly that Grayson's prime asset, his dead-ball accuracy, would prove the decisive factor in his favour. 'I rate the importance of goal-kicking very, very highly,' the coach said. 'We've got to go to Australia with a minimum of two world-class kickers. The team that lifts the World Cup will be the one that wins the tight games, and that might come down to one kick. You've got to have guys with a proven track record.'

> 'I think I underrated Grayson then because we all knew Wilkinson was a fantastic player.'
>
> *CLIVE WOODWARD*

Grayson certainly had a proven track record. He was third on the England all-time points-scoring list with 314 from 25 tests, behind only Wilkinson and Rob Andrew. Thirteen of those points had been vital in helping England to their impressive 9–23 win over the New Zealand Maoris in difficult kicking conditions in June. In contrast, King had missed six kicks at goal against the Welsh.

The writing appeared to be on the wall for King, and Woodward was not about to give him any reassurance in another interview. Nearly four years after the last World Cup, the England coach now admitted that he had made a mistake in his handling of Grayson and Wilkinson in that tournament's crucial group game against New Zealand. 'If I had my time again I would have played Grayson at ten and Wilkinson at twelve,' he conceded. 'I don't think Jonny was ready to play in the fly-half position in games of that magnitude. He should certainly have been in the team, at twelve, where he was playing his club rugby. I think I underrated Grayson then because we all knew Wilkinson was a fantastic player. Grayson would have kicked those goals against the All Blacks.' For his part, after a four-year absence from the international stage, Grayson wasn't prepared to let his second chance slip by. 'I was fairly disillusioned with life, but now, as things have worked out, I'm desperate to make the World Cup,' he explained. 'I'll do everything within my power to be on that plane.'

At the England training camp in Aix-en-Provence, Wilkinson, who would be rested again for the France match, remembered the 1999 tournament as a heartbreaking experience. 'That New Zealand game was the be-all and end-all to me,' he said. 'I found it a very nerve-racking occasion and it definitely took its toll. I accept that both on and off the field I could and should have done things differently. I made a number of wrong decisions because I didn't play with my head up enough to see what was happening. I grew tired as the game went on and, because things weren't going right, I felt as if I was butting my head against a brick wall. At the time it was the most intense game of rugby I'd ever played in.'

However, typically, the negatives of that defeat and his relegation to the reserves' bench for England's losing quarter-final against the South Africans were turned into positives by Wilkinson. 'There's a big difference between me at twenty, and me at twenty-four,' he revealed. 'I'm far more at ease with myself and with what this game is all about. I realise I don't have to get every single thing exactly right all of the time. I'm learning more and more to express myself as a player, and to impose my personality on the game. I'm actually enjoying my rugby now, which is something I couldn't honestly say in the past.'

Clearly, though, the level of enjoyment he gets from the game is highly dependent on results: 'I'm very pleased to have helped win the Grand Slam at long last, and to have achieved everything else that I have in the game, but it doesn't really matter right now. Disappointment or ecstasy, failure or success, it's all going to rest on the next few weeks. In that sense the past is totally irrelevant.'

The other significant selection for the France game was Iain Balshaw. As a young star, Balshaw had shone brightly during the 2001 Six Nations campaign, but then his (along with quite a few others') confidence had seemingly been shattered by the 2001 Lions tour to Australia. Operations on both shoulders – one following a dislocation, the other requiring complete reconstruction – plus an ankle with two torn ligaments then served to knock the Bath full-back further down the pecking order. But Woodward and his management team had never lost faith that the boy from Blackburn would rediscover his form and his natural talent to run with the ball. Even though it had been twenty-two months since he had last started for England (in the ill-fated Grand Slam attempt in Dublin in autumn 2001), and although he had played little more than a dozen games in two seasons, 'Balsh' now had the chance to cement his place in the England World Cup squad.

'I was beginning to think someone didn't want me to play rugby any more,' he admitted, when looking back over nearly two years. 'I became a real couch potato, sat at home watching TV with my arm in a sling and foot in a cast. Now I realise that getting injured was the best thing that could have happened to me. I'd had five or six years without any kind of a break. To get injured meant that I could step back from rugby and chill out a bit. I had analysed myself too much. The more I watched the videotapes, the worse I'd get.'

'I was beginning to think someone didn't want me to play rugby any more. I became a real couch potato, sat at home watching TV with my arm in a sling and foot in a cast.'

IAIN BALSHAW

Now Balshaw saw his chance to return Down Under, and this time make his mark. 'I'd love to go back to Australia and play as I should have done the first time around,' he said. 'The blame for that Lions experience comes down to me. It was the opportunity of a lifetime, and I didn't take it. There was too much analysis of things for my liking. For me, it's a question of being spontaneous. Since that experience, and especially now that I've shaken off the injuries, it's been a case of getting back to how it used to be, playing spontaneously, doing the basics and knowing that everything else will fall into place. In the past I used to take opportunities that came my way. That's what I've gone back to. I'm as relaxed now as I was when I first came to Bath. As for Saturday, I'm not apprehensive at all. I'm bored of not playing. I can't wait.'

Woodward was delighted to see Balshaw back. 'The biggest thing is that he is fit and looking good,' he explained. 'It is now up to him to show what he can do and we will know come Saturday night. I am not a shrink and I do not know about him for sure. The Lions tour was too long ago and it does not help that it keeps being brought up. It is up to us to make sure he is at his best.'

England would suffer a minor setback midweek when they were forced to make a back-row change after the Wasps number eight, Joe Worsley, twisted an ankle in training. Sale's Alex Sanderson would take his place in the back row, with Gloucester's uncapped flanker Andy Hazell promoted to the bench.

The French, meanwhile, named a powerful side to play their old rivals in front of a sell-out, 60,000 crowd. In the past three years France had defeated New Zealand, Australia and South Africa in Marseille. With the World Cup now just six weeks away, and with the possibility of a Sydney semi-final against England, defeat at home was not an option for France. So the French head coach, Bernard Laporte, despite claiming that he wanted to try out all thirty of his World Cup squad, opted for his strongest line-up. The only change from the side which had comfortably brushed aside Romania 56–8 in Lens the previous Friday was at full-back, where Nicholas Brusque would come in for the injured Pepita Elhorga.

Nevertheless, 'There is no such thing as a first or second team,' insisted the French manager, Jo Maso. 'We are still evaluating the whole group. After all, this is not a Six Nations or even a proper Test match.' Of course, his words were far from supported by Laporte's team selection.

While Maso was playing down the match, the formidable French flanker Olivier Magne was talking it up. 'France versus England can never be referred to as a friendly,' he announced. 'It's bigger than anything. But we have the Vélodrome. It's in Marseille that you feel you are among rugby connoisseurs. More so than in Paris. The crowd really gets into it and their proximity to the pitch means that their fervour is passed on to us.'

And so it proved on the Saturday night. But, although France recorded a win over England by the narrowest of margins, the visitors left Marseille with a great deal of pride intact. With maybe three exceptions (Cohen, Lewsey and Tindall), Woodward had put out a team of reserves, or even second reserves. To have come so close against the French first team proved yet again that England's strength in depth was unmatched anywhere in world rugby.

The defeat may have brought to an end England's record run of fourteen consecutive victories, leaving the team just three short of New Zealand's and South Africa's jointly held record of successive international wins, but it was easy to shake off any disappointment. The England second fifteen had pushed the French first fifteen all the way, and could quite easily have won, if either of Grayson's two injury-time drop-goal attempts had made it over. No wonder the French celebrated as if they had just won the World Cup when the final whistle blew.

However, while England received a confidence boost in defeat, few of the individuals on the field of play did enough to suggest that they were certainties for Australia. Probably the only two exceptions were Grayson and Martin Corry, who followed up an impressive display in Cardiff with an even better one in Marseille, and was making a compelling argument for inclusion in the final thirty. Austin Healey, in testing circumstances, was not given the opportunity to shine at scrum-half and still looked a step or two behind Gomarsall, while Balshaw hobbled off just after half-time before being able to prove himself. There were definite flaws, too, in the England performance, notably in the line-out, where five English throws were lost and another two were so poorly controlled that Healey could make nothing of them.

Any notion that this might be a friendly warm-up was dispelled within a minute of the start, by which time opposing props Julian White and Jean-Jacques Crenca had both trotted off the pitch with blood injuries. The partisan crowd had been riled even before the start, when Phil Larder, England's defensive coach, had stood his ground as the French Foreign Legion band had marched down the middle of the pitch. Instead of removing himself from the fray, Larder had forced the bandsmen to march around him. Cue a hail of boos from the stands.

Although a Frederic Michalak penalty gave France an early lead, Grayson, who had earlier missed a drop goal, slotted home an equalising 9th-minute penalty amid a cacophony of deafening jeers. England, wearing their new, figure-hugging, skin-tight shirts for the first time, then took a deserved lead nine minutes later when Corry caught a line-out, was driven forward by his pack and left an inviting gap for the strong Mike Tindall to exploit. Tindall still had work to do after receiving a pass from Grayson, but he shrugged off a tackle to touch down. 'To be honest, the good work from Martin Corry and then Paul Grayson didn't make it hard for me to finish the move off,' Tindall declared modestly. Having scored the try that crushed Ireland in the Grand Slam-clinching win in Dublin, then another vital one in Melbourne against the Wallabies, the big Bath centre, not renowned as a prolific scorer, had clearly struck a rich vein of form.

With Grayson converting the try, it was beginning to look like England's night. Then, two minutes later, they looked as if they might run away with it. Lewis Moody went on a trademark burst to set up an excellent opportunity in front of the French posts, and Grayson chipped to the left-hand corner. It looked perfect for Iain Balshaw to win the race and touch down, but the full-back was judged to have been offside. 'It would have been a great

Above: the long hot summer of 2003. Jason Leonard and Trevor Woodman relax in an ice bath at Bagshot after training (*David Rogers/Getty Images*).
Below: Andy Gomarsall leads another England attack against Wales (*John Gichigi/Getty Images*).

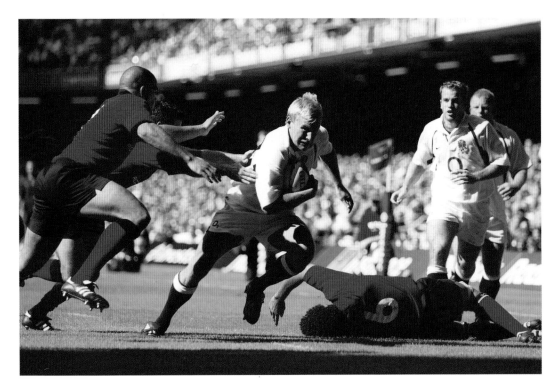

Stuart Abbott (above) and Joe Worsely contribute to the demolition of Wales in Cardiff, August 23rd (*both David Rogers/Getty Images*).

Above: Dorian 'Nobby' West, England's new captain for the first 'friendly' against France, in Marseille. *Below:* Lewis Moody breaks away from France's Christophe Dominici (*both David Rogers/Getty Images*).

Both Simon Shaw (above) and Austin Healey (here caught following a collision with a TV camera) were (initially) unfortunate to miss out on the final 30. Martin Corry's exceptional form saw him board the plane for Australia (*both David Rogers/ Getty Images*).

Mike Tindall celebrates another crucial try (*David Rogers/Getty Images*).

Martin Johnson's final World Cup. The captain adjusts his headgear in training, and leads the team out in the final fixture before Perth, against France at Twickenham (*both David Rogers/Getty Images*).

'I've scored a few more memorable than that one.' Ben Cohen on his opening try at Twickenham (*Mike Hewitt/Getty Images*).

Iain Balshaw, back to his very best, accelerates past Clement Poutrenaud to score (*David Rogers/Getty Images*).

'I couldn't have cared less about the last World Cup.' The thoughts of Rugby League star Jason Robinson back in 1999 (*David Rogers/Getty Images*).

Another try against France and England fans are left in a state of high expectation prior to Australia (*Mike Hewitt/Getty Images*).

way to have celebrated my comeback,' admitted a rueful Balshaw later. 'And, of course, it would have meant an England win, too.'

Reprieved, France then began to answer back, but only after a tense Michalak had missed two penalties. The fly-half slotted a drop goal six minutes before the break to reduce the arrears, and then France took the lead for the first time in the game two minutes later. Their try came from a turnover of an English ball, which allowed four sprinting French backs to bear down on two English defenders. Jauzion provided the last pass to Brusque, who touched down in the corner. In doing so, the new French full-back just evaded a gallant attempt by Ben Cohen to halt him. A moment of controversy or farce, depending on one's point of view, then followed, when England's baggage man, Dave 'Reg' Tennison, on a mission for his physio-therapists, ran out across the line of Michalak's kick moments before the stand-off missed the target. Cue more jeers from the crowd.

'I had to smile when I saw it,' admitted Woodward later. 'Dave didn't know what he was doing and I wish the kick had gone over, but there you go. You just had to laugh about it and say it was one of our better moves in the match. But I do apologise profusely for what happened. I don't think any coach in their right mind would plan anything like that.' Tennison pleaded his innocence, too: 'I had no idea that the French player was lining up a conversion,' he insisted. 'I was just concentrating on organising the drinks for the players because it was close to half-time.' Michalak should have been allowed to take the kick again, but he was not. The incident provided one of the major talking points from the match afterwards.

> 'I had to smile when I saw it. Dave didn't know what he was doing and I wish the kick had gone over.'
>
> CLIVE WOODWARD

In the few minutes after Michalak's conversion miss there was more controversy as Alex Sanderson charged down a French clearance but just failed to control his touchdown. The South African referee, Mark Laurence, was able to make the decision of no-try only after he had consulted with Welsh video referee Huw Watkins.

In injury-time at the end of the first half Grayson and Michalak swapped penalties to hand France a 14–13 lead at the break. They almost increased it three minutes into the second half, but Brusque's touchdown in the corner from a cross-field punt had occurred after his body had gone into touch. Once again, it was Watkins who made the decision.

Then Balshaw's ill-luck continued. First, when it looked odds-on that he would collect from Lewsey's cross-kick to score, the ball took a wicked bounce to deny him; then, a minute later, he injured his leg. 'It's nothing too serious,' he would report afterwards. 'Certainly nothing compared to what I've been through in the past couple of years. But I could have done without it tonight. I don't think I've done enough yet to convince anyone of my place in the World Cup.'

Balshaw's night was in marked contrast to Grayson's. When West was replaced by Steve Thompson, the fly-half took over the captaincy and then slotted his third successful penalty to give England the lead. However, Michalak responded again in the 64th minute with a kick that crept over via the right-hand post. This seemed to spur France into action and England were subjected to a barrage of attacks which they managed to repel sometimes only with desperate, last-ditch tackles. France were kept out but, crucially, England failed to score again themselves, although Grayson went desperately close with those two injury-time drop-goal attempts. The first was charged down by France's South African replacement centre, Brian Liebenberg, while the second missed by a matter of inches from forty metres out.

In spite of his fine individual performance, and the honour of captaining England, Grayson was anything but happy after the final whistle. 'I'm not pleased at all,' he declared. 'The sheer will to play for England and perform is contagious. Ultimately, we all played to win, we had the opportunities to do so, we made it difficult for ourselves, but still we could have won, but ended up failing to do so.'

Mike Tindall was of a similar view. 'I'm very deflated, as we all are,' he explained, his leg strapped and iced to ease a strained calf muscle that would most likely rule him out of facing the French a week later at Twickenham. 'It's a harsh world and it was dire in the dressing room. Some of the boys in there had this down as their last shot at World Cup selection. We let ourselves down and we played awfully. Losing is bad enough, but the way we lost makes it worse. We'd have been very lucky to have come away with a win.

'If we can't win scrum and line-out ball, we can't go forward. This was a great chance of beating them in their own backyard, where they had never lost, but we threw it away. We had a really good shot at the world record of consecutive test wins and it hurts to have lost that run. We never saw it as a lesser England team, or any kind of damage-limitation exercise. We were confident of a victory and, as events have proved tonight, we could and maybe should have achieved just that.'

Austin Healey knew his personal contribution had left him right on the edge of selection but, considering the year he had just endured, he remained philosophical. 'It was just great to play, especially after being told by a surgeon that I'd never play again,' he said. 'I was told just one hour after coming round from the anaesthetic. I only knew two weeks ago that I would be able to play again, so to be able to wear the England shirt was very special. I'm just grateful for the faith Clive has shown in me.'

A disappointed Woodward lamented the loss of control in set plays but was able to see the value of the match through his disappointment. 'What bugged me is that we got outmanoeuvred at the line-out,' he said. 'If the line-out and scrum had gone to normal standards, we'd have won the game, but you're not going to win those games without the ball. The French out-played us in the line-out. We just seemed slow. With a more experienced team in certain positions we may not have made the tactical errors we did. You can get carried away sometimes when you see teams score forty to fifty points against Wales. In reality, that's not going to win us the World Cup. We learned far more than we did against the Welsh.'

And the coach was determined to put those lessons into practice: 'Selection has become far more straightforward than it was. We'll have a different team for the return game in a week's time at Twickenham. If everyone's fit, all the main guns will play. These guys are gagging for a game. There's no point trying to protect people like Jonny Wilkinson. He's a rugby player and he needs to play. If he doesn't, his head will explode.'

As he headed off into the warm South of France night, Woodward made one final, revealing comment: 'We have to be very hard-nosed about it now,' he said. 'The World Cup is just around the corner, and we've got to take tried and tested players.'

> 'He's a rugby player and he needs to play. If he doesn't, his head will explode.'
>
> *CLIVE WOODWARD on JONNY WILKINSON*

Just how hard-nosed he was prepared to be was revealed within twenty-four hours, when eight of the forty-three-man squad were struck off the World Cup list. Bath lock Steve Borthwick paid the price for his part in the line-out failure in Marseille; as did Alex Sanderson, who, given an unexpected chance as a result of Joe Worsley's twisted ankle, failed to take it. Newcastle centre Jamie Noon, who had played the full eighty minutes against Wales and the last half-hour against France, also failed to make the cut. His club colleague, fly-half Dave Walder, would join him back on Tyneside. The Leeds full-back Dan Scarborough, who was capped against Wales, was out, along with Wasps prop Will Green, uncapped Gloucester flanker Andy Hazell and the Sale hooker, Andy Titterell.

'I had to make some tough decisions but I have made these earlier than I intended in order to give the players as much notice as possible so they could prepare for the Zurich Premiership with their clubs,' Woodward explained. 'All eight players have been outstanding in their attitude on and off the field.

They are all young players who have a future with the England squad. I have not made any decisions regarding the five other players who will not be travelling to Australia with the final thirty.'

So, one final warm-up international to go, and five players to be omitted at the final hurdle. The heat had suddenly been turned up to maximum.

Chapter 3

ENGLAND   45–14   FRANCE

Saturday 6 September
at Twickenham

England: Robinson, Balshaw, Greenwood, Abbott (Lewsey, 60), Cohen, Wilkinson (Grayson, 43), Bracken (Dawson, 33), Woodman, Thompson (West, 73), White (Leonard, 67), Johnson (Captain; Shaw, 43), Kay, Hill, Back, Corry (Moody, 57)

Tries: Cohen 2, Robinson, Balshaw, Lewsey
Cons: Wilkinson 3, Grayson
Pens: Wilkinson 4

France: Poitrenaud, Garbajosa, Jauzion, Liebenberg, Dominici (Rougerie, 40), Merceron, Yachvili, Milloud, Ibanez (Captain; Bru, 70), Poux (Marconnet, 73), Auradou, Brouzet (Pelous, 58), Chabal (Magne, 51), Tabacco (Harinordoquy, 63), Labit

Try: Rougerie
Pens: Merceron 2
Drop Goal: Jauzion

Referee: N. Williams (Wales)

Attendance: 75,000

France knew that their hard-won victory in Marseille could provoke a very strong reaction, and their suspicions proved to be correct. 'This means *l'enfer*,' admitted Raphael Ibanez, the victorious French captain, as he considered the rematch in the dressing room at the Stade Vélodrome. 'In English you say "hell". It could be hell for us at Twickenham. With this victory I think we had a very big present from England. For them it would be a disaster to lose at home now.'

After just one day back at home, the England team reassembled at the Pennyhill Park Hotel in preparation for England–France II. When the team was finally announced twenty-four hours after the usual Monday press conference – Woodward had wanted to give Tindall, Balshaw and Lawrence Dallaglio every chance to recover from their injuries – Tindall and Dallaglio were both absent, while Balshaw was selected for the bench. Of the generally assumed 'first fifteen', only Phil Vickery and Josh Lewsey were also missing. The Gloucester loose head was suffering from a groin strain and would be replaced by Julian White, who, it was fair to say, was very eager to have another go at the French. 'The last game was, from a front-row point of view, frustrating, but also character-building,' the prop said. 'The French were disruptive, but we were a bit naïve. Personally, I was very disappointed by the night. We props have our egos and you don't like it when it's not going well. We were aware of what was going on and it was up to us to sort it out.'

On the wing, Dan Luger would start, although Balshaw was likely to come on the field at some point. However, Woodward left no one in any doubt about his first choice: 'I want to make it clear that Josh Lewsey will be going to the World Cup,' he confirmed, making the Wasps winger and full-back his first public selection, even ahead of Wilkinson. 'I have decided to pick Dan Luger and put Iain Balshaw on the bench because we want to have another look at them.'

Woodward had opted to return Jason Robinson to full-back to allow Luger another run-out following his strong showing against Wales. It would now be in Luger's hands to secure a squad place. Gloucester's James Simpson-Daniel, ruled out for this game alongside Joe Worsley, Alex King and Mark Regan, who all had minor injuries, was Luger's main rival for the position.

Elsewhere, Martin Johnson was back at captain, Neil Back, Richard Hill and Ben Kay would be unleashed, and, in the backs, Jonny Wilkinson would be playing his first game of the new season, with Will Greenwood outside him and Kyran Bracken at scrum-half. 'Kyran was outstanding on the summer tour and I have gone with him, although the rivalry with Matt is as intense as ever,' Woodward explained. Bracken and Dawson had been fighting for the number-nine jersey, with almost equal success and almost identical international records, for nine years now, and each knew that he could never consider the position his by right.

'We're now almost past the trial stage,' continued Woodward. 'It's just a question of dotting the "i"s and crossing the "t"s. I've got an ideal model in my mind of the various numbers in each unit I'm going to take to Australia. Sometimes, though, people's form can make you see it differently.'

Wilkinson confessed to suffering from itchy feet: 'I've been desperate to play,' he said. 'I don't like watching and I also want to find out for real just where I am in my preparation. Only playing will tell you that. The list of things I have in my mind now to work on will be different by Saturday night. It's been a while since I last played, and with a World Cup just around the corner you just want to get a run.'

Although Wilkinson hadn't enjoyed the public vote of confidence that Woodward had given Josh Lewsey, only a madman would have thought that his place on the plane Down Under was in any doubt. Others in the team were under far more pressure, though. Martin Corry, the Leicester forward who usually plays in the back row but is also accomplished at lock, had been on a long journey from has-been to the brink of the England World Cup squad. International rugby had been hard to come by since he had won his first cap back in 1997 against Argentina. Indeed, this would be his first start for England at Twickenham. After a successful tour of Australia with the Lions in 2001, the Leicester Tiger had lost his way to such an extent that he hadn't even been a member of England's second team in the spring. Corry, though, had refused to abandon hope. 'I was on the bench for the England "A" team, so you'd have to say I was not in contention for the World Cup,' he admitted. 'I'm not hiding the fact that it has always been a massive battle for me, but I have drawn strength from that.' Corry's re-emergence was perhaps the biggest surprise of the late summer. This was his third outing in as many weeks, and if he put in anything like the performances he'd displayed in Cardiff and Marseille Woodward would have a real selection dilemma on his hands. Could Corry oust his club colleague Lewis Moody from the final thirty? Or would the coach dispense with a fourth lock in the squad in favour of Corry, which would mean that Simon Shaw, who had done little wrong, would miss out?

Corry said, 'This is just like *Fame Academy*. You're all working away and

> 'This is just like *Fame Academy*. You're all working away and flogging your guts out together...You are still good mates. It's very hard when you see guys left out.'
>
> MARTIN CORRY

flogging your guts out together. While you're in competition with one another, the intensity builds a rapport. You are still good mates. It's very hard when you see guys left out. I know how much a World Cup place means to me, so I know how much it means to them. At times like that you just want to be left alone to reflect. It's really hard to take, but that's the nature of the sport. Now, for me, it all comes down to Saturday.'

Woodward conceded, 'Martin's done very well so far. He's had two outstanding performances and is pushing very hard, but so are others. The key is that we don't shrink from the tough decisions. Some outstanding players will be left behind. I know now at the back of my mind who is going to make it.'

Another player fighting for a place on the plane was Stuart Abbott, who would be winning his second cap after his try-scoring debut against Wales. The former South African Under-21 and Western Province centre qualified for England through his English mother. In May 2003 the Springbok coach, Rudi Straueli, had contacted Abbott in the hope that he could be persuaded to join the South African squad, but Abbott had declined the invitation on the off-chance that he might make it with England some day. At that stage, he had not been picked for the end-of-season tour to Australia and New Zealand. Now he had the opportunity to edge in front of Ollie Smith for the third centre's place behind Greenwood and Tindall. 'This is a great chance for me to show that I can step up,' he said on hearing of his selection. Ironically, he would be finding himself directly opposite another South African, Brian Liebenberg, who would be making his full debut for France. 'Stuart Abbott deserves this opportunity and it is a big chance for the World Cup,' said Woodward.

Then, just when everyone had fully assessed the implications of the team selection, everything changed, certainly behind the scrum. Dan Luger strained his back during a gym session and was forced to withdraw. It was clearly a blow to the newly signed Perpignan winger's hopes of making the final cut, and suddenly made Iain Balshaw's selection for the World Cup much more likely. The Bath man was promoted to the starting fifteen against France, with Josh Lewsey moving up to the bench.

Even more surprising than the Luger/Balshaw situation, though, was the news that emerged about Alex King and Mike Catt. The former had to withdraw from consideration for the World Cup through injury, and the latter was asked to join the squad to replace him. 'I haven't picked Catt yet, just asked him to come for fitness tests,' Woodward explained. 'Then we'll do it on merit.'

King's eleventh-hour exit was a cruel twist of fate, his World Cup dreams shattered by the costliest injury of his career. His knee, damaged during the Welsh win a fortnight earlier, had deteriorated to such an extent that the doctors were now convinced the Wasps fly-half would not recover in time to play a part Down Under. King was understandably distraught as he bade farewell to the rest of the squad and headed off for more scans and consultations.

'Alex was devastated, but honest enough to agree that he would not be ready in time,' said Woodward. 'The doctor felt it wasn't right after training on Wednesday afternoon. If he had come through I don't think I would have called up Catt, but I do need three guys in the squad who can all play at number ten.'

Martin Johnson expressed his sympathy for King. 'It's gutting for Alex to have got this far and then have to pull out,' said the England captain. 'The boys really feel for him. But the whole point of having this squad together – we've been in camp for six of the last seven weeks – is so that someone can slot straight in. That's the way it is with injuries. You can't worry about them. They happen and you've got to be ready for them.'

One man's loss was another's gain, of course. But in this case it was a very unlikely man who benefited, for Mike Catt had played the last of his fifty-six tests for England in the win over South Africa in November 2001 before losing his place in the centre to Mike Tindall. Equally adept at fly-half or inside centre, the Bath player's late arrival on the scene just four days before the final thirty would be announced suddenly gave Woodward fresh options.

Catt, who was nearly thirty-two, had made only eleven starts in 2002/3, his year blighted by a persistent hamstring injury. 'He shouldn't have been playing at all and I told him that there was no way I would pick him until he got himself into condition,' Woodward revealed. 'There has never been any hidden agenda. I have probably been in touch with him more than any other player. The theme we have used is that it's not over until the fat lady sings. I don't think he did himself any favours last season by playing when he wasn't fit. I told him categorically: "Your only chance of making the World Cup is to have a complete summer's rest, get yourself in great physical shape for pre-season and I'll come and watch you play." That's exactly what happened. He went away and got into shape.'

Woodward then travelled down to Pontypridd to see Catt play for Bath in a pre-season friendly, and also watched tapes of him in action in other looseners against Exeter and Henley. Clearly he had seen enough to justify the call-up, although, of course, this did not guarantee Catt's inclusion in the final squad. 'This is fantastic news for me,' Catt said on receiving the head coach's call late on the Wednesday evening. 'It brings me a step closer, but nothing is set in stone. Now it's a question of whether they pick me. It's great to be part of the squad and it's something I've worked exceptionally hard for.' It also ended weeks of speculation for Catt over whether he had any kind of international future.

Just as England had used several fringe players the week before, France now decided to give their second fifteen the chance to push for a call-up to the first team, although there would still be a number of world-class players running on to the Twickenham turf. The back three of Clement Poitrenaud, Christophe Dominici and Xavier Garbajosa have terrorised defences all over the world for many years and would be sure to punish England if given the chance, while their colleagues would be desperate to prove some points.

'This is our chance to show the coach we're good enough to make the first team,' said the Toulouse number eight Christian Labit, the understudy to Imanol Harinordoquy.

'If we're not up to the physical challenge, then we face a major disappointment,' added Garbajosa. 'Everybody tells us that it will be a war, but that's fine. That's how you create solidarity and strength in a squad.'

At least the French all knew they would be on the World Cup plane. It was different for several of the peripheral England players, especially as the announcement of the final thirty would not be made until the day *after* the France game. The pressure on them in the build-up to the game (not to mention the match itself) was enormous, and the tension cannot have been eased by the fact that it was obvious where Woodward's chief dilemmas lay: which of Iain Balshaw, Dan Luger and James Simpson-Daniel would lose out in the back three? Would it be Stuart Abbott or Ollie Smith in the centre as back-up to Will Greenwood and Mike Tindall? Would Mike Catt burst his way in as a utility back? Would Andy Gomarsall win the battle with Austin Healey for the third scrum-half place behind Dawson and Bracken? And would Woodward pick three locks and six back-row players, or four and five, respectively? This final decision would be of great interest to the likes of Graham Rowntree, Simon Shaw, Martin Corry and Lewis Moody.

Corry had been in a similar situation before, and vividly recalled the phone call he received from Andy Robinson to be told he had not made the initial Lions squad for the 2001 tour to Australia. He was intent on doing his best against France, of course, but knew the next morning would be a difficult time as he waited for Woodward's call. 'The first thing you see is the name flash up on your mobile,' he explained. 'It's the call you've been waiting for and your heart's in your mouth. You start to sweat and your heartbeat rises. When Andy Robinson phoned me he started off by barely saying anything. He certainly didn't get down to talking about final selection, but I could tell it was bad news just by the tone of his voice. He didn't enjoy making the call. He knew it meant a lot to me and that I'd be gutted if I'd failed to make the squad. It will be the same this time as well. I'll know instantly just by the tone of Clive's voice. I'm not great to talk to at the best of times, but I'll be terrible company on Sunday waiting for that call. I'll try to busy myself, but the hours of waiting will seem like days and the minutes like hours.'

Corry was adamant that he would make the effort to do the right thing if he wasn't selected: 'I won't be able to do it immediately,' he said. 'I'll need a good couple of hours to sulk first. But then I'll get on the phone to congratulate the players [who were selected]. It will hurt like hell to do so, but I'll do it.'

Lewis Moody, who had recovered from injury to push hard for a place, had a similar view on life. 'I don't want to hear about me being young and that there are other World Cups for me,' he said. 'It's all about now and this World Cup. I'm desperate to go, and I'll be very, very disappointed if I don't. In fact, if the truth be known, I'll be devastated. You try to subdue your nerves and get on with training and life within the England camp, but the thought of Clive's phone call is always lurking there in the back of your mind. It's been an incredibly stressful week. It's like waiting for your "A" level results, but worse.'

> '**I don't want to hear about me being young and that there are other World Cups for me. It's all about now and this World Cup. I'm desperate to go.**'
>
> *LEWIS MOODY*

Andy Gomarsall, too, was feeling the pressure. 'I'll be completely and utterly gutted if I don't make it,' said the Gloucester scrum-half. 'I don't want to be overdramatic, but the phone call could be a major factor in the whole of my career. I suppose it's the same in life for a lot of people. One phone call could set you up for life in business. It's the same for me.'

Martin Johnson, of course, did not face the same fears: as captain, he knew, barring last-minute injury, that he would be playing in his third and last World Cup. But he still felt for those who were hoping to join him and would miss out: 'It's going to be tough for the rest of us to see five players go, but it's going to be a hundred times tougher for them,' he conceded. 'It was bad enough when the first eight were told to leave after the French defeat last weekend. At least they were told at home. They didn't have to come to the team hotel, and we didn't have to watch them pack their bags. Then the remaining squad members were, to a man, devastated for Alex King when he left us during the week. He'd been playing and training so well.

'Now we face the final cut. Whoever goes would have been training hard with us all summer, totally committed to the World Cup cause. They will be classy internationals, certainly good enough to go. It's just that thirty-five into thirty won't go. It's not even going to boil down to deciding who's better than whom. Ultimately, it will come down to what permutation Clive comes up with to create a balanced squad.

'The only thing I can do is remind those who miss out that it's still not definitely over for any of them. We have nearly four weeks to go before we leave for Australia, and anything can happen during this time. Then we have four pool games and, hopefully, three knock-out games as well at the World Cup. Anyone can get injured, and anyone could get called up.'

Thankfully, no one was injured on Saturday night. Instead, England made the most impressive of points having lost to the French the week before by staging a near-perfect World Cup leaving party that saw a record post-war win. Indeed, at times, especially during the first half, England were awesome in the way they dismissed France.

Led by the irrepressible Martin Johnson, with Jonny Wilkinson inflicting maximum damage with his left boot (and surging past 700 international points in the process), Ben Cohen proving why he is the deadliest finisher in the world and Jason Robinson causing his customary mayhem, England humiliated an opposition who had high hopes themselves of lifting the World Cup. It was only in the second half, when Woodward made a series of substitutions, that England eased off the gas. By then, the damage had been done. Sporting eleven members of the team who captured their first ever win in Australia in June, England were understandably hungry. Having suffered the end of their sequence of consecutive test victories the previous week, they were determined to keep the run going for consecutive *home* victories (it stood at an impressive twenty-one before the match). If that wasn't motivation enough, some of the players knew that their place on the plane to Australia might be won in the eighty minutes against France, and they played like it. The end result was that England turned in one of the finest displays seen at headquarters for many a year.

The night began with a rendition of 'Swing Low' from UB40, followed by a prolonged cheer of appreciation from the capacity crowd as the England players scampered on to the pitch. The roar was both a celebration of their endeavours in New Zealand and Australia in June and a good-luck message before the start of the World Cup.

Amid all this English euphoria, ironically France grabbed a 3rd-minute lead through a Gerald Merceron penalty. But three minutes later Wilkinson had struck the first of three rapid-fire penalties to ease England into a 9–3 lead, the platform from which Ben Cohen would launch himself at the French line.

After a scrummage had developed into a couple of quick, driving rucks in England's favour, Wilkinson's 33rd-minute grubber kick headed towards the French posts. Will Greenwood looked as if he might make it to the ball, but Dimitri Yachvilli got there first, only to make a complete hash of his clearance, flipping the ball on to a post. The rebound allowed Cohen to touch down for one of the easier tries of his career. 'I've scored a few more memorable than that one,' he would admit later with a smile. 'But they all count, especially when it's the first try against a team as strong as France.'

Just three minutes later Cohen was the beneficiary once again after a move involving two beautifully weighted passes from Wilkinson and Greenwood. Cohen burst through a fragile-looking French defence on a perfect angle to record his 23rd try in just his 29th international. As French heads dropped, Jason Robinson took full advantage in first-half injury-time by darting through the narrowest of gaps with a customary jink and a sprint along the left touchline to place England out of sight at 33–3. Yet again, the former rugby league star had proved why he is considered the best player in the world at beating opponents from a standing start.

By now Kyran Bracken had been replaced by Matt Dawson. The former had experienced one of those heart-in-mouth moments when he had felt a twinge in his back as he warmed up on the tackle bags before the game. Bracken had missed the whole of the 1999 World Cup with a long-running back injury and was in such despair at the time that he had even sought help from Eileen Drewery, Glenn Hoddle's faith healer. This time he at least made it on to the pitch and got through thirty-three minutes, before being dragged from the field by the England team doctor Simon Kemp, who had attempted to sideline the scrum-half a few minutes earlier, only to be swatted away.

'Neil Back reckoned that was one of the best tackles of the day when the doc got me off,' said Bracken. 'I was gutted when I felt the back go. It went into a spasm after I hit the tackle bag awkwardly. It was there all the time but not bad enough to prevent me from starting. I'd been rooming with Alex King for the past fortnight and when he had to withdraw from World Cup contention in midweek it brought back sad memories for me. The last World Cup was a time of torment. So, fingers crossed I will not have any problem. I've got to nurse myself and make sure I'm fit for the World Cup. I'd be devastated if I missed another one.'

His rivalry with Dawson explained his very public reluctance to leave the field. 'You never want to give an opponent like Matt the chance to come on,' he admitted. 'He is a colleague, but he is vying for the same shirt and we both want to wear it. When the doc came on I thought I had a few minutes left to finish the half, but he told me: "You're coming off whether you like it or not."'

If France were looking for some

> 'Fingers crossed I will not have any problem. I've got to nurse myself and make sure I'm fit for the World Cup.'
>
> *KYRAN BRACKEN*

second-half respite, it took just nine seconds to shatter that hope. In that time Iain Balshaw gathered Wilkinson's kick-off after a mistake by Sebastian Chabal and scampered over to score in the corner after a typically mazy run in and out of a circle of French defenders. Given an opportunity through Luger's withdrawal, the Bath player had grabbed it with aplomb, reminding everyone of the talent he possesses when fit. 'I just wanted to last the eighty minutes,' he said afterwards. 'I've done everything I can now to get into the squad. I'll admit I was a little concerned last week when I came off injured in Marseille. The nature of the injury worried me, as did whether I'd done enough to prove myself. But now I'm happy. If I don't get selected, at least I've given it my best shot.' Later, Woodward said, 'I was very pleased with Iain. He proved how well he can play for England,' which sounded like Balshaw's best shot had been good enough.

Almost as soon as Balshaw had touched the ball down, Woodward took off his two irreplaceables: Johnson, possibly making his final appearance at Twickenham, and Wilkinson. 'No point exposing them to potential injury when the game was won and the job done,' Woodward explained later. This gave Simon Shaw a final opportunity, and Paul Grayson some extra practice. Lewis Moody then came on as well to replace a clearly tired Martin Corry, who, after three test matches in three weeks, had given his all in his bid to make the World Cup squad. Six minutes later, on trundled Jason Leonard to win his 106th test cap for England, and his 111th in total, if you add the five he has earned as a Lion. That took him level with world record-holder Philippe Sella, although purists will insist on Leonard winning all 111 in an England shirt before granting him the tie. 'I wasn't aware of equalling that mark until someone told me,' Leonard confessed later.

> ## 'I wasn't aware of equalling that mark until someone told me.'
>
> *JASON LEONARD*
> *on his record 111th test cap*

Understandably, given all the changes, England's momentum stuttered, and France, mindful of the embarrassing nature of the margin, kicked a second penalty through Merceron in the 55th minute amid a barrage of jeers from the crowd. Then, in a damage-limitation exercise which worked to a degree, they brought on some of their big guns in Aurelien Rougerie, Olivier Magne and Imanol Harinordoquy. Cohen would, as a result, be required to make three try-saving tackles on Rougerie, Chabal and finally, the best of all, Ibanez. The French hooker had been just a metre from the line when Cohen collared him.

In the end, France managed to put some more points on the scoreboard. Centre Yannick Jauzion dropped a late goal, then two tries in injury-time rounded off a thoroughly entertaining encounter. First Josh Lewsey, on for the impressive Stuart Abbott, was given a clear run to the line after Neil Back had provided the final pass. Then Rougerie finally crossed England's line for a consolation try in the corner with seconds remaining. It would prove to be too little and much too late for a rather beleaguered-looking French team.

After the setback in Marseille the week before, Clive Woodward was smiling again, content to get an emphatic victory under his belt before setting off for Australia, and relieved that he didn't have to make any last-minute adjustments to his squad. 'Nobody's gone backwards from tonight's game,' he announced. 'I knew my squad before and nothing's changed. I'm now very clear in my own mind who they are. I was just happy to get back to winning ways and to emerge unscathed in terms of injuries. We wanted to win badly. The game was over by half-time and it was an excellent win over the top side, along with ourselves, from the Northern Hemisphere.'

Nevertheless, as defensive coach Phil Larder would admit, this time it was the opposition who were not showing their full hand. 'France did not ask as many questions as they normally would,' he said. 'Come the World Cup, they will be far more dangerous.'

Indeed they would, but for now this was the least of England's concerns, and certainly was far from the thoughts of the dozen or so players who faced a sleepless night, not knowing whether they would be spending October and November in Australia or at home in England. All would be revealed the following day.

Chapter 4

THE SQUAD

Clive Woodward announced his final thirty on the Sunday as planned, having sent text messages to his big guns to tell them they were in the squad, as expected. He spoke personally to the five who missed out and to those who had been waiting on tenterhooks before receiving the nod.

Possibly the most startling inclusion was Mike Catt, who, having joined the squad just four days earlier, now found himself on his way to the World Cup. His selection, plus that of scrum-half Andy Gomarsall, meant that there was no place for Austin Healey. Martin Corry's valiant efforts proved not to be in vain, but his selection as a result of his versatility in the back five meant that lock Simon Shaw, who could not have done much more in the warm-up internationals to prove himself, was desperately unlucky to miss out. With six back-rowers now, Woodward also opted for just four props, when most had expected five. This meant an unhappy telephone call for Graham Rowntree, who had played in all five games during the Grand Slam, and had served England so well during the heroic test win in New Zealand just three months earlier, especially when he was one of the six remaining pack members on the field against eight All Black forwards. 'It is very, very tough on Graham,' admitted the England scrum coach, Phil Keith-Roach. Healey, Rowntree and Shaw have all been Lions in their time, which served to underline the extraordinary strength in depth at Woodward's disposal.

'It's particularly tough on Austin and I've had a long chat with him,' Woodward explained. 'He has had almost a year out and, although he has done very well, he has not quite done enough to be selected. In a squad like this you need three people who can play at number ten, especially when you consider the tough pool matches we have to play and who we may face in the knockout stages. Clearly we've got two in Jonny Wilkinson and Paul Grayson. Mike Catt is the next person in after losing Charlie Hodgson and Alex King. Once Alex was injured it became a simple choice. The thing everyone has to get into their minds is that we're not taking a squad of utility players. We must have the best twenty-two available in each position for the key games. So, although Catt can play centre, he will be training to play fly-half.'

Healey, who always suspected he was fighting a losing battle against time, was most philosophical. 'Of course I'm disappointed,' he said, 'but you have

'The thing everyone has to get into their minds is that we're not taking a squad of utility players. We must have the best twenty-two available in each position for the key games.'

CLIVE WOODWARD

to put it in perspective. When I came round from the anaesthetic for my knee operation there was the surgeon telling me that my career was over. So this pales into insignificance alongside that. My wife is expecting our second child this week and I've got the joy of clocking on for duty at Leicester at nine a.m. on Monday morning. Going back to the club to get ready for the Zurich Premiership is the best way to channel all the frustrations into something positive. This is not about me, it's about England going Down Under and trying to win the World Cup. In some ways I had prepared myself for bad news. I played in the hardest game, against France in Marseille, but ultimately time just caught up with me. I wouldn't wish injury on anyone, but Clive has told me I will be covering nine, ten and the wing. I will make sure I am prepared if anything unfortunate does happen.'

Matt Dawson has been a close friend of Healey's for many years. 'I know exactly how much Austin has put into coming back from two serious injuries last season to put himself in a position to challenge for the World Cup squad,' the scrum-half said. 'It's been a long, hard summer of lonely rehab and fitness work even before he rejoined England at the team hotel. I also know exactly how much pride he takes in wearing the England shirt and how it will be killing him not to be involved. And, among other things, I am badly going to miss my main cribbage partner. There's absolutely nothing you can say to offer any consolation to Austin, or the others, all superb rugby players and top blokes. Since the 1999 World Cup I've dreamed and thought about little else than the 2003 World Cup and being part of an England squad for Australia. It would have been exactly the same for the five who missed out.'

When it came to the forwards, Woodward had found it very difficult to break the news to the unfortunate Rowntree and Shaw. 'They were the two hardest decisions I've had to make in my six years as head coach,' he said. 'Shaw could not have done more to deserve inclusion. He was devastated when I spoke to him. He is an outstanding person to work with, but it came down to the balance of the squad. The same is true of Rowntree, but I had to be practical, and Martin Corry has been playing exceptionally well. He's been named in the back row, but I have no doubt he can play at top level in the second row if called upon to do so. The decision I've gone with wasn't necessarily the one I would have gone with six weeks ago. That's why I was delighted we had those warm-up games. Regarding the remaining five players who didn't make it, they have all made a significant contribution to England being successful. It was just that the competition within the squad was huge.'

Martin Corry had not suffered for too long on Sunday morning before hearing the good news. 'I was staying overnight at the England team hotel and came downstairs with my wife for breakfast early after a disturbed night, then I saw Clive sitting in the restaurant,' he explained. 'I thought it would be politic to sit well away from him, but, within moments of us sitting down, Clive came across the room to tell me that I'd made it. Breakfast suddenly became an extremely enjoyable meal. I can really empathise with the other guys, though. I've been there myself so I know how much it hurts. As to what's my best position, it doesn't really faze me any more. Back row is where I've played most of my rugby, but I feel comfortable at second row, too.'

Mike Catt – who as a result of his dramatic comeback had seen his nickname change from 'Catty' to 'Lazarus' – had more cause for celebration than any of his team-mates. As recently as the previous May even walking was rarely pain-free for the Bath player. 'What I needed was two or three months off, but Bath were struggling, and my job, along with those of twenty-one other guys, was on the line,' Catt said. 'So, every six weeks, I would try to get back. There were times when I felt I was over those injuries, and then, three weeks later, I would end up pulling the other one or the same one again. It was very hard because we were fighting at the bottom of the league. I didn't communicate with Clive during that period. I was distraught trying to sort out my body and, to be fair, he didn't want anything to do with me because of my injuries.'

Woodward confirmed Catt's analysis. 'I wasn't best pleased with what he did last season,' said the head coach. 'He wasn't doing himself any good playing for his club while injured. Every time I went to watch him I came away shaking my head. I saw a player whom I knew was world class who was unable to perform anywhere near his best.'

After Woodward had given Catt an ultimatum the Bath player wondered whether the World Cup would pass him by, especially when he stayed at home training and rehabilitating while others toured Australia, New Zealand and North America. Then, of course, he was not even named in Woodward's initial forty-three. 'I always knew, though, that if I could sort myself out physically that mentally I was still definitely capable of playing internationally,' revealed Catt.

He did not dispute that when he finally got the call-up to the World Cup squad he owed much to the ill-fortune of Hodgson and King: 'There is some luck involved, of course, but I've been around long enough to know that things do happen. Rugby's a very fickle sport and people get injured or left out all the time. I've worked extremely hard for it and it has been a lonely ride, especially when nobody wants you.'

In the end, the choice became relatively easy for Woodward. 'Between Catt and Healey, Catt is a far better, more experienced guy if we need him to start at number ten against Georgia or South Africa. Of the two, I'd go with Catt hands down. He's been lucky, but that's what sport is about. You make your own luck, and we're very lucky to be able to call on him now.'

Few would have begrudged Catt his moment of joy, especially after the off-field torment he had endured over the previous year. He had come close to losing both his wife Ali and baby daughter Evie. It was an experience that forced him to 'grow up', and appreciate the stresses England team-mates Will Greenwood and Ben Cohen must have suffered. The trauma of Ali's emergency Caesarean section and the subsequent open-heart surgery Evie underwent have transformed Catt from the selfish, intense individual he suggests he was into a man able to see the value of a life away from the game. 'I've been very, very lucky in life,' he said. 'I've never had any real trauma, never lost any family member, and although I've felt sorry for others who have, I've never really understood. At least, not until now.'

While three-week-old Evie fought for life, Catt admitted he 'was trying to be Mister Tough Guy, which is why there was a delayed reaction. I might have been able to handle one trauma, but to have two so close to each other was too much. The worst period for me was four months after it had all happened. That's when I really struggled. The reaction kicked in hard. That's why I have so much respect for Ben and Will, and a little more understanding, too, for their experiences of losing Ben's father and Will's baby boy. I was lucky. It all ended happily for me and everything's all right, although it was so, so close to being just terrible. The way Ben and Will coped with their personal problems and have been able to focus on their rugby is very impressive. I went the other way, though, and lost myself a little. It was just the thought of me sitting at home on my own, if I had lost both Ali and Evie.'

> 'My family will watch me in Australia and my little girl will soon be able to run about a rugby pitch. I couldn't be happier than I am right now.'
>
> *MIKE CATT*

Off and on the field Catt is consequently a new man. 'To get to the top in most things you have to be a little selfish and I've certainly been guilty of that at times,' he admitted. 'Now I understand people a lot more and I've chilled out. I no longer dwell on rugby, but move on. I used to be so intense and probably wasn't much fun to live with. I certainly prefer the me of today to the me of a couple of years ago. My family will watch me in Australia and my little girl will soon be able to run about a rugby pitch. I couldn't be happier than I am right now.'

Completing the selections in the backs line, Stuart Abbott beat Ollie Smith to the final place in the centre, while Iain Balshaw's re-emergence and Dan Luger's greater experience and proven try-scoring record saw them nudge out James Simpson-Daniel on the wing. For both Smith and Simpson-Daniel, two young stars of the future, their time will undoubtedly come, although this would have seemed like scant consolation on that Sunday morning.

A relieved Dan Luger insisted after receiving the thumbs-up from the management that those who were not selected should not now be forgotten. 'We want to win the World Cup now as much for the guys who missed out as for ourselves,' he said. 'They have worked every bit as hard as the rest of us to get England to this point and we owe it to them. We have got an opportunity to do something that when we are older we can tell our children and grandchildren about. And there is a real chance of that happening. It's not just that we are in the World Cup and we might do it, we have a definite chance to do something special.'

This was especially true for Luger himself. He had gone from first-fifteen certainty to fringe member of the squad through little fault of his own. With 22 tries to his name in just 34 tests, he was fifth in the all-time England tries record list, but he would surely have scored many more had it not been for a series of serious injuries. 'There was a time when these things first happened when they seemed like the end of the world,' he admitted, 'but I've become more philosophical about it and you only have to look around to see it's not just me. There are guys who are ahead of me, but I'm in the squad and it's up to me to take the chances when they come my way.'

Clive Woodward, though remaining understandably cautious, reflected that England's prospects were now extremely exciting. 'A lot of people have labelled us as favourites,' he conceded. 'It's not a statement I'm scared of. It's bound to happen if you look at our recent results. I think we are favourites, too, along with the All Blacks. Andy Robinson and I never really felt we had the chance when we played to be the best in the world. That's all we're trying to do here. So we won't be going into our shells. I can't remember too much of the detail about our preparations for the 1999 World Cup, but I do remember losing. You don't forget those experiences, and that will keep our feet firmly on the floor. If someone had said to me four years ago, just after we'd been knocked out by South Africa in the quarter-finals, that we would be in this position as the favourites, or joint-favourites, I would have been very surprised. There are no guarantees, but our job is to put the team into a position where they have a chance of winning it.

'All we can talk about now is the next game and, of course, we have a great chance of beating Georgia. By the time we get to Australia, the amount of coaching we want to do is minimal. The heavy work will be done here. We want the load to be light in Australia, precise, and the players to be fresh in body and mind.'

Former England captain Lawrence Dallaglio was of a similar view. 'It is difficult to give ourselves a target other than winning the competition, but come what may we have to play to our potential when we get to Australia,' he insisted. 'Over the last twelve months that is what we have done and we know it will take a very good side to beat us. If you have a record like ours, of course people will be looking at you. With what has been achieved over the past three or four years, and particularly the last year, you cannot get away from the expectation, enthusiasm and interest from rugby fans and also people outside rugby.'

Steve Thompson had been in the fortunate position of never really doubting his World Cup selection. Over a twenty-month period he had played in eighteen test matches and emerged from virtual obscurity to become arguably the best hooker in the world, a view endorsed by Martin Johnson: 'He's the hooker England have been looking for over the past couple of years,' said the England captain. Phil Keith-Roach agreed: 'He's got quick feet in the scrum, which is why he's able to strike cleanly,' said the scrum coach. 'He's remarkably uncomplicated. He's found his own system that works. You can cover your eyes when some club front-row forwards get the ball deep in their own half and move the ball forward, but you want Steve to get the ball. He's a natural. He finds places where no one has coached him to go. And it works. He's like a bulb in the garden. He's just grown and grown of his own accord.'

The Northampton Saint himself said, 'I really feel more comfortable in myself these days, and more confident, too. I know I shouldn't say so, but my debut season in the Six Nations was a horrendous experience. I was so scared. But then we went to Argentina and came away with a win. That was a big moment. Now I feel I'm really taking part in games, not just doing the basics.'

> 'He's like a bulb in the garden. He's just grown and grown of his own accord.'
>
> *PHIL KEITH-ROACH on STEVE THOMPSON*

Thompson's front-row colleague, Trevor Woodman, acknowledged the role Jason Leonard has played in his elevation to first choice loose head for the World Cup after so many years waiting for the venerable Harlequin to bow out of international rugby. 'I have learned so much from Jason, watching him in action and playing against him at club level,' the twenty-seven-year-old Gloucester prop revealed. 'I've studied how he handles himself off and on the field and made notes which I have used to improve. The man is a fantastic player who has the utter respect of team-mates and opponents alike. Ask any front-row player from around the world and they'll only have compliments, however grudging. My problem was that I would play one or two great games but then drift off as I admired previous efforts. Jason has proved that you need six or seven games in a row to stay in possession of the jersey. I knew I had to achieve that and believe I did. The number-one jersey is my reward.'

Further back in the scrum, Neil Back spoke of his dreams. 'You don't have to be a football fan to know that England won the World Cup in 1966,' he pointed out. 'Names like Hurst, Moore and Charlton are forever linked with greatness by people who never even saw them play. How I would love to add my name to that roll and in doing so leave a similar legacy for my two children. As they grow older, newspaper cuttings and videotapes will be their only means of recalling what their dad did. How proud I would be for them to be able to say I was a World Cup-winner.

'Back-to-back European Cups I won with Leicester, numerous Five and Six Nations titles and a Grand Slam with England are all fantastic memories for me. So too are the domestic leagues and cups I have picked up with Leicester, a triumphant tour with the 1997 Lions and historic England victories this year in New Zealand and Australia. But the World Cup is the tournament you want on your record, the achievement you want your name to be associated with for ever. It is the ultimate prize in sport. I remember saying to myself before my first World Cup in 1995 that, whatever happened, there would be further opportunities because age was on my side. I can no longer say that.'

Two of the superstars of the England team were equally frank in their assessments prior to leaving for Australia. For Jason Robinson, a rugby union World Cup represented uncharted waters, because back in 1999 he was still playing rugby league for Wigan. 'I could not have cared less about the last World Cup because I was brought up in rugby league and was totally ignorant of union,' he admitted. 'When I think back to 1999 and consider where I am and what is expected of us, it's astonishing.

'When I look around the England squad, I have this marvellous sense of security. It is very special to know deep down you are surrounded by guys who definitely can do the job and a management that is able to make it happen. England have the talent, ambition and quality to achieve something memorable here. This is a team who can win anywhere, any time. Knowing that is extra special. This is the biggest sporting challenge of my career and, if we do go on to win the World Cup, then it will overshadow everything else I have achieved.'

Like Robinson, Jonny Wilkinson was a vital component in a team that won all over the world, but he was in no doubt that October and November in Australia will be a step further, even for him. 'Pressure doesn't come any greater than in a competition which everyone wants so badly to win,' explained the England vice-captain. 'There is something special about putting yourself under the biggest spotlight. You play the game to get to the pinnacle. You put your whole life into it, as I have done, and all that effort is channelled into the biggest tournament. Winning it would mean every-

> **'This team goes to Australia knowing it has no excuses.'**
>
> *CLIVE WOODWARD*

thing. When I look around the dressing room at the rest of the players just before we go out, I know I can rely on every one of them. So we are desperate to do well and we know that if we perform to our potential we are capable of beating any team.'

As the day loomed for departure and the long flight to Australia, the final words, quite rightly, were left to the head coach and his captain. For Clive Woodward, every working day since 1997 had been leading up to this moment. 'I would swap five Grand Slams for one World Cup,' he claimed. 'Beating the other teams in Europe cannot compare with overcoming the best the world can offer. I have never said that England will win the World Cup, only that we *can* win the World Cup. This team goes to Australia knowing it has no excuses. I would not swap one of my coaches for a New Zealander or an Australian. Not one. And in Andy Robinson I have the best coach in the world. Together I believe we have transformed England's rugby. Now we are asking them to surpass themselves. Like Olympic athletes, they are being challenged to produce new personal bests on the biggest stage of all. If we do that and it is not enough we will be able to live with ourselves. Defeat would only haunt us if we fell below the standards we are setting ourselves.'

According to Martin Johnson, the rugby world had changed markedly since the last World Cup. 'We weren't good enough to win it last time, it's as simple as that,' he conceded. 'And I'll tell you one of the main reasons why this was so: we were all guilty of getting it out of proportion; the players, the management, everyone involved. We got it out of kilter, we made it too big. I can tell you now that most of the guys didn't even enjoy the 1999 tournament, and not just because we were dumped out of it by the Springboks.

'Now, I just think the whole team's managed to put some perspective on life, especially those who have suffered private grief in recent times. A lot of the guys have been through some tough times off the field and it's helped us all to understand that, as desperate as we are to win the World Cup, life goes on whatever. Whether I return as the captain of the world champions or not,

I'll still have my wife and my daughter, hopefully my health and the rest of my life to look forward to. I'm not saying I won't be bothered – I've put my heart and soul into winning this World Cup – but I've gained some perspective in my life which I maybe didn't have four years ago. As a result of all this, I know that the squad's going to enjoy this World Cup much more than last time, whatever happens to us. We're going to be more relaxed, we'll make sure we have some fun during each week before games and try to get rugby out of our heads for a while.'

Like Woodward, the captain believed that England had a favourite's chance: 'We know all the opposition well now and we've already proved that we can beat them in the sort of games that will lead us to winning the final. We know we have the ability and I have the confidence in my team to believe we can win the World Cup. Maybe last time we *hoped* we would win it. This time we're going to Australia *knowing* we can win it. If we don't succeed, we'll be massively dejected. I would imagine it would be the biggest disappointment of my career if we fail. We're going to need some luck, be relatively injury-free, get the right bounce of the ball on occasions, the right refereeing decisions and everything else that a world champion requires. If we get that, then there are no excuses.'

On a personal level, Johnson expressed the pride he now feels when pulling on the white jersey: 'You appreciate playing for England much more when you know it's coming to an end,' he explained. 'I've been guilty of taking it all for granted earlier in my career, as we've all been. But I've had a few quiet moments recently when I've reminded myself that this is it, this is my last chance, and that I have to throw all my energy into helping England win the World Cup. If I'd been told in the mid-1990s I'd be leading England in the 2003 World Cup, I wouldn't have believed it. In fact, even after the 2001 Lions tour I couldn't see it happening. But when you're winning, rugby is fun; and you don't feel the injuries as much, either. I've no idea whether I'll carry on with England after the World Cup. It's a decision to be made then, not now. Right now my concern is winning the World Cup. I can't say we'll win the World Cup, because nobody knows for sure. But I can say we have a hell of a good chance and we're ready. This time we're ready.'

Johnson would find himself the centre of attention from virtually the moment he and the rest of the England squad first set foot in Perth. The South African captain, Corne Krige, had referred to the England captain as 'one of the dirtiest captains in world rugby', which was inflammatory, to say the least, with the crucial World Cup pool match between England and South Africa just a fortnight away. Considering Krige's own role in the violent clash at Twickenham the previous November, his comment raised more than a few eyebrows.

However, mindful to avoid a repeat of the Twickenham bloodbath in

> 'You appreciate playing for England much more when you know it's coming to an end.'
>
> *MARTIN JOHNSON*

Perth, Krige soon backtracked: 'It was irresponsible on my part to have said these things,' he said, insisting that the comment had been made as an aside after an interview with a South African journalist had officially ended. 'I hadn't expected to see those words in the paper. I don't want to say what I really do or don't believe about Johnson, except to say that he's an extremely good player.'

The England coach laughed off suggestions that Krige's comments would have riled Johnson and the rest of the squad. 'A few years ago it might have done, but now we smile about it,' Woodward responded. 'We get so used to it. It's not just Krige. It's a lot of coaches and players, whoever we play against. I call it positive feedback. It's going to come for the weeks that we are here. It's part of the baggage you carry for being part of the England rugby team. We know that we can't do anything about it. It's up to me every now and again to fire a few barrages back, and when I do everyone goes mad. If you saw the reaction in the players' team room, you'd understand it's quite amusing. I'd be very annoyed if any of the England players ever retaliated.'

Besides, never mind South Africa, for the time being England had to focus all their attention on Georgia. Naturally, everyone expected the minnows to be overcome, but the burly men from Eastern Europe certainly had the potential to pose a few problems in the first World Cup pool game, which was now just a week away.

Chapter 5

ENGLAND 84–6 GEORGIA

**Saturday 11 October
at the Subiaco Oval, Perth**

England: Lewsey, Robinson, Tindall (Luger, 38), Greenwood, Cohen, Wilkinson (Grayson, 48), Dawson (Gomarsall, 38), Woodman (Leonard, 30–32), Thompson (Regan, 41), Vickery (Leonard, 52), Johnson (Captain), Kay, Hill (Moody, 52), Back, Dallaglio

Tries: Cohen 2, Greenwood 2, Tindall, Dawson, Thompson, Back, Dallaglio, Regan, Robinson, Luger
Cons: Wilkinson 5, Grayson 4
Pens: Wilkinson 2

Georgia: Khamashuridze (Khekhelashvili, 80), Urjukashvili, Zibzidadze, Giorgadze, Katsadze (Captain), Jimsheladze (Kvirikashvili, 80), Abuseridze, Shvelidze, Giogadze (Dadunashvili, 77), Margvelashvili, Didebulidze (Nadiradze, 45–48, 52), Labadze, Yachvili (Bolgashvili, 71), Chkhaidze (Machkhaneli, 85)

Pens: Urjukashvili, Jimsheladze

Referee: P. de Luca (Argentina)
Attendance: 25,501

MATCH STATISTICS
Possession: England 77%, Georgia 23%
Territory: England 77%, Georgia 23%
Scrums Won: England 11, Georgia 7
Line-outs Won: England 8, Georgia 5
Rucks/Mauls Won: England 110, Georgia 28
Tackles Won (Attempted): England 40 (41), Georgia 154 (194)

It had been some time since England had last faced an opposition virtually unknown to them (and indeed to the rest of the rugby world), but Georgia were precisely that. There was never any doubt that England would win this match, and win it well, but how good would Georgia be, what kind of a contest would they give the English, and did they have the potential to become a power in the game?

If nothing else, this and the other matches on the first weekend of the World Cup would underline how wide the gulf is between the Englands and Australias of the world and the likes of Georgia, Uruguay and Namibia. While no expense had been spared to get England to Australia in prime condition, the Georgians had had both their training camp in the Caucasus and a planned tour of Canada cancelled due to lack of funds. In the end, they had set up a makeshift camp in France, where seventy-five Georgians play their rugby. The Georgian national team's track-suits had come courtesy of the generosity of their French coach, Claude Saurel, and other officials, who had clubbed together to buy them. Moreover, there is only one scrum machine in all of Georgia, only eight rugby pitches, and just over three hundred adult players. Yet, in an opinion poll, Georgians overwhelmingly said that rugby was the sport in which their country had the greatest chance of success. Forty-two per cent plumped for it, compared with only 27 per cent for wrestling, a sport in which Georgia regularly wins Olympic medals. Football was in single figures. When Georgia played Russia in the Rugby European Nations Cup some 65,000 packed into the national stadium in Tbilisi, and another 44,000 watched Georgia beat Russia again to qualify for the World Cup. The lower figure was explained by the fact that there was live television coverage of the match, but it was still 24,000 higher than the attendance at the previous day's Georgia–Russia football international.

Part of this support for the game rests on the fact that the national pastime, lelo (after which the Georgian rugby team takes its nickname of the 'Lelos'), is vaguely similar to rugby. It's a ferocious ball-game dating back to medieval times and played between neighbouring villages. The referee is usually an Orthodox priest.

In spite of Claude Saurel's presence at the head of the Georgian team, the historic links between the two nations and the French training camp, relations between France and Georgia had not been totally cordial in the build-up to the World Cup. Three of the seventy-five Georgians based in France had been refused permission to play in the competition by their clubs. All were suspended by the French Federation for the duration of the tournament. Another five had, in effect, been sacked, and arrived in Australia as free agents. On an allowance of just thirteen pounds a day for seventy days, all would obviously end up considerably out of pocket.

'We are light years behind England, but we realise there's nothing much we can do,' said Gregoire Yachvili, the Georgian flanker (although he was born in France), whose brother Dimitri was the reserve French scrum-half. 'We might not have tackle bags, body armour or a scrum machine, but at least we have a ball and a pitch.' They also had ingenuity: 'We have some home-made [scrum] machines which you can create with an old Soviet tractor and some good ideas,' explained Zaza Kassachvili, the Georgian RFU vice-president.

> **'We have some home-made [scrum] machines which you can create with an old Soviet tractor and some good ideas.'**
>
> *ZAZA KASSACHVILI,*
> *the Georgian RFU vice-president*

All of this was a world away from the meticulous English preparation, of course, but one part of that preparation was unlikely to be as thorough as usual: the scouting report. It's not quite as easy to find hours of videotape footage about Georgia as it is for the All Blacks or Springboks, so to some extent England were in the dark about the opposition. There was, however, one exception. Vano Nadiradze, at six-foot-four the tallest man in the team, had already battled it out with Martin Johnson *et al.* in a Heineken Cup clash the previous season, scoring a try for Beziers against Leicester in the process. 'That was a good match for me,' said the thirty-one-year-old. 'This time it will be a very physical contest with Johnson and the other England players and we are ready. Everyone in the Georgia team has to do his duty for eighty minutes, particularly in defence. We have to concentrate on defending against the English. This is the key.'

England, meanwhile, named their first squad selection of the World Cup five days before the Sunday-evening match. The only slight surprise was that Woodward was starting his strongest team, rather than keeping anyone in reserve for the next match, against South Africa. Matt Dawson won the nod at scrum-half, narrowly edging ahead of Kyran Bracken in their ongoing battle for possession of the number-nine jersey, although Woodward was at great pains to point out that he now saw very little between Dawson and Bracken (who had seemed to be in poll position over the summer). Nor, indeed, did he put either of them far ahead of Andy Gomarsall. 'Dawson and Bracken are both fully fit and available for selection and there is no daylight between them any more,' said the head coach. 'In fact, all three of my scrum-halves are world class, and this is just my first pick of the tournament.'

Elsewhere, Phil Vickery, Lawrence Dallaglio and Josh Lewsey all returned to start after their various ailments. Julian White, Martin Corry and Stuart

Abbott, who had all started against France at Twickenham, would miss out. According to Woodward, Lewsey's return had been threatened by the re-emergence of Iain Balshaw, a sign that no one in this England team could rest on their laurels. 'Iain was close to getting a start and I would like to think that he'll have a big role to play,' the head coach revealed. 'He looks in great shape and is back to his best. He's certainly putting pressure on the back three positions.'

The strength of the England team was explained by the fact that Woodward wanted to give his first-choice players a good run-out before the stiffer challenge that awaited them six days later. 'In the back of my mind I've always been planning it this way, ever since I saw the draw,' he explained. 'The majority of those players have played only once in four months, so it is important that we start strongly.'

As for Georgia, Woodward was certainly not taking their threat lightly. In their last warm-up game, a 31–22 loss to Italy in Asti, the men from Eastern Europe had pushed the Italians all the way until an explosive last few minutes saw one Georgian sent off and another sin-binned. 'A lot of these guys ply their trade in French club rugby, so we expect it to be tempestuous,' the head coach admitted. 'I don't think for one second it will be a rout. I believe it will be a good start to the World Cup.'

Andy Robinson had a particular interest in the Georgian pack. 'They are very hard boys,' said the forwards coach. 'The one thing we know is that they are built for scrummaging. Looking at their recent Italy and Russia games, they put a lot of store by that and we are expecting a physical contest up front. I don't think it will turn into a fight, just good, hard, physical rugby. We will go in with a lot of respect for their scrummage.'

Josh Lewsey was more knowledgeable about the Georgians than most, having come across them a number of times in international sevens competitions. 'They're great athletes,' he confirmed. 'On the sevens circuit they've scalped Fiji, Ireland, Scotland and Wales. The surprise is how quickly they have improved against the top nations.'

While Woodward was of course most concerned with his team selection and keeping his players motivated, a distraction came in the form of the latest verbal attack launched towards England. John Muggleton, the Australian defensive coach, put forward his opinion of the number of thirty-somethings in the English squad. 'Their medical staff will be working overtime with them, and the coaches will have to make compromises in training,' said Muggleton of Messrs Johnson, Back and others.

Woodward was exasperated. 'It is amazing how many coaches of other teams still want to talk about England,' he said. 'We have Australia about to play Argentina and yet that's what they want to do. We are so used to it we smile, take it on board and say nothing. I don't know the age of the Australian forwards and I don't care. All I know is that we have a very good squad.'

Anyway, according to twenty-five-year-old Steve Thompson, the older guys in the team were proving to be the fittest. 'They tend to beat me in fitness tests,' the hooker revealed. 'You see some of them running around like lunatics and they are probably playing the best rugby they've ever played in the past year. Physically we have had the best preparation we have ever had. I have worked harder than I have ever worked before, and that is precisely because players such as Martin Johnson and Jason Leonard are driving me forward. It is an easy stick to beat us with, and if it was not this thing about age it would be something else.'

Jonny Wilkinson, meanwhile, revealed how his latest high-profile friend had been in contact to send his best wishes to the England squad. Prior to leaving for Australia, Wilkinson had teamed up with David Beckham to shoot a television commercial, and apparently 'David has been very supportive, which is fantastic.' The Adidas commercial was doing plenty to raise the stand-off's own profile back in England, but he seemed unaffected by the heightened interest in him and his new pal. 'Flattery and acclaim don't motivate me. I have my own ambitions and set out my stall to try to meet them every time I play. So now I'm just desperately keen to get going, and keen to make the most of the time I've got. This is so important to us that it's bound to cause nervousness.'

'It's a huge match for us because it's all about England making a statement of intent,' explained Neil Back. 'It's about us showing the rest of the teams in the tournament what we're made of and that we mean business. It's about us being physically ruthless. It's about us making the world and his wife sit up and take notice. It's about us laying down a marker about the way we can play rugby. Anything less will give our rivals reason to doubt us, our critics ammunition to fire at us, and the Springboks cause for confidence ahead of next week's game. I don't want Georgia crossing our try line. I don't want us coming off the Subiaco Oval at the end of eighty minutes feeling that we underperformed. That has been my message to the team in the build-up.'

'We're all a bit edgy in that we just want to get out there now and play,' revealed Jason Robinson. 'I'm hoping to be able to leave a lasting impression. The big games are the ones that you dream of, the ones that you get a buzz from. We did well in the summer when we won in New Zealand and Australia, but now we've got to go that one step further.'

On the Thursday morning England

> **'It's about us making the world and his wife sit up and take notice. It's about us laying down a marker about the way we can play rugby.'**
>
> *NEIL BACK*

had the slightest of scares when Dawson and Balshaw were both forced to sit out training because of general muscular soreness. Dawson would recover in time for the game, but Balshaw would be forced to withdraw from the reserves' bench, allowing Dan Luger into the twenty-two.

Alongside Luger on the bench would be England's (and the world's) most experienced international. If he got a run-out on the pitch at any stage, he would set a new world record for test appearances, as well as appearing in his fourth World Cup. The prop was well aware of the differences between this current England squad and its predecessors at earlier World Cups. 'The feeling in 1991 [when England lost in the final to Australia] was that we were a good team, especially at home, and could win, providing the opposition had a bad day, we got the bounce of the ball, the weather was in our favour and we had a little bit of luck,' he said. 'It was a case of having to find external help to give us the edge against other top teams. Now, though, this England team is not reliant on home advantage or anything else to win games. The attitude we are taking into the World Cup is very simple: this is the way we are going to play, no matter who we face. We have total belief in ourselves.'

On the Thursday evening Martin Johnson and Corne Krige, along with all the teams in Pool C, came together for a capping ceremony in King's Park, Perth. Handshakes were made all round (Johnson and Krige's was somewhat curt) before photographs were taken. Asked later what he felt of Krige's earlier salvo, Johnson replied casually, 'It's not really on our radar screens at all. You can get involved in slanging matches. I can't be bothered.'

He was prepared to comment on the expected physical nature of the World Cup, however. 'Mention the word "physical" and people think about foul play. Physical play is what rugby union is all about – commitment, big hits, big tackles, hard but fair contact. For this reason, the laws are strict. You operate on the very edge of those at the highest level, but what matters is staying on the right side of legal. If people do things on the pitch they shouldn't do, they're going to get caught. There are too many cameras, too many officials. By all accounts, this is going to be a very strict World Cup. That is fine by us, providing it is the same for everyone.'

On Georgia, Johnson remained respectful, having managed to get hold of at least some film of the opponents: 'This is a strong and physical team, big guys with huge pride and an understandable anxiety to make a big impression in their first game in a World Cup. If I had to compare them with one of the more familiar sides we face, I'd say Georgia remind me most of France.'

At least the meeting of the teams in King's Park seemed to break the ice with South Africa, according to Woodward. Having shaken hands with both Krige and coach Rudi Straeuli, he declared: 'I had a few polite words with

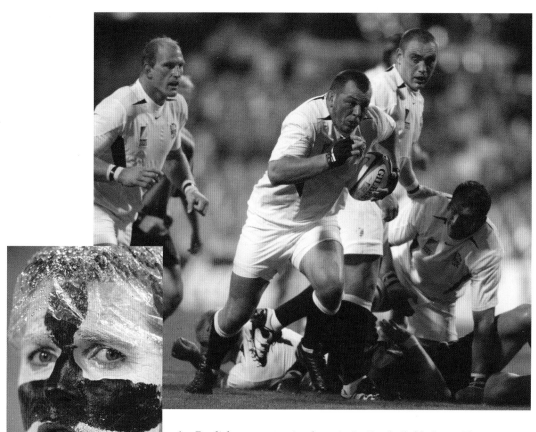

An English supporter in the rain in Perth (left). Steve Thompson (above) was crucial to England's first victory in the World Cup, over Georgia ... as was Neil Back (below) *(Chris McGrath/David Rogers/Getty Images)*.

Will Greenwood (above) and Ben Cohen (below; both v Georgia) in the midst of their own competition to be the leading try scorer (*both David Rogers/Getty Images*).

Oppostie
Jonny Wilkinson's penalties saw England through against South Africa (*David Rogers/Getty Images*).

Captain Martin Johnson takes on Bakkies Botha (below left), while Jonny Wilkinson comes smack up against the Springbok defence (below right, *both David Rogers/Getty Images*).

Opposite
'The first touch was Goater-style ... I nudged it, and the next thing it hit the back of the net.' Will Greenwood on his crucial breakthrough try against South Africa (*David Rogers/Getty Images*).

Jason Robinson (above) and Joe
Worsley (right) take a battering from
Samoa; but finally England break
through with a Neil Back try (below;
all David Rogers/Getty Images).

Relief as England finally pull ahead –
courtesy of a brilliantly worked try
between Jonny Wilkinson and Iain
Balshaw (above); Dan Luger's 34
seconds on the pitch (below) prove
costly, resulting in a two-match ban for
fitness coach Dave Reddin (right) and a
£10,000 fine for the RFU (*all shots
David Rogers/Getty Images*).

The England maul takes on Uruguay (above, *Darren England/Getty Images*); and Andy Gomarsall (below left), with two tries, and (right) Josh Lewsey, with five, are among the scorers (*Darren England/Jon Buckle/Getty Images*).

them. It was interesting meeting them, but that is not going to have any bearing on next week. It just proves that rugby does have this fundamental ethos which is excellent. If I'm honest, I don't think either the England or South Africa players were too comfortable being there. There was obviously a bit of tension between the sides.'

Friday was the last day when the England team could relax. Mindful of Johnson's promise that this time the players would ensure that the World Cup would not get to them, they attended a beach party in Perth, socialised with the crowd, signed autographs and built sand-castles. While across the city the Australian batsman Matthew Hayden was rewriting the cricket record books by scoring 380 against Zimbabwe, the England players were treated to an Aboriginal dance performance on the shore of the Indian Ocean, the symbolic purpose of which was to protect the visitors from evil spirits during their stay in Australia. Matt Dawson spoke for all the squad when he declared that personal agendas and individual hopes did not exist within the England set-up. 'I've not been involved in many sides that have been like that,' he admitted. 'The Lions in 1997 had it, and certain Northampton teams, too. But it's the first time it's happened since I've been with England.'

Dawson himself had given his all for this moment. 'There are those close to me who would say the World Cup has virtually taken me over,' he confessed. 'I'm determined to spare nothing over the coming weeks. I've put too much effort in over the years and made too many sacrifices not to do myself justice.'

And that would begin against Georgia. The scrum-half was keen to point out that, despite the bookmakers' odds indicating that it was among the most one-sided matches in history, England were not taking their opponents lightly. 'We're treating Georgia with maximum respect,' he said. 'First, it would be an insult to them if we did otherwise and, second, only by doing that can we perform to our maximum. If we are to become world champions, we must play every game like world champions.

'So it has been business as usual. We've changed nothing in our pre-match preparations for this week. It has worked brilliantly for us over the past eighteen months, so why change now? Team sessions every morning, personal training in the afternoon, the day off forty-eight hours before kick-off and then the match itself.'

Lawrence Dallaglio reiterated his and his team-mates' intentions, starting with Georgia. 'We will go up a level from where we've been for the past twelve months,' he insisted. 'We all understand that if we want to win the World Cup, we have to reach another level. As for four years ago, when myself, Neil Back and Richard Hill were again the back row used, there is no comparison between then and now. There has been a massive change since then, all over English rugby. Everyone is that much more experienced, and the Premiership clubs much more professional. We have better coaches, the players are fitter and skill levels are up. I haven't played a game for a while, but I don't feel at all rusty because we've been working very hard. There's no substitute for playing your first match, but it's been very game-related in training.'

Come the morning of the match, the routines for the two teams could not have been more different. While Jonny Wilkinson, for example, went through his painstakingly meticulous preparations, the Georgians all attended morning service at Perth's Russian Orthodox church. Afterwards, Zaza Kassachvili spoke of his concern that his players might pay England too much respect. 'What might our boys do when they finally meet Jonny Wilkinson?' he asked. 'Maybe they want to shake his hand and say hello. I hope not. The mothers, fathers and godfathers of Georgian rugby are waiting for this game. We don't know what will happen. We hope the baby is beautiful. There is an impression that Georgia will maybe kill someone. This won't happen. We will play with respect.'

'The mothers, fathers and godfathers of Georgian rugby are waiting for this game. We don't know what will happen. We hope the baby is beautiful.'

ZAZA KASSACHVILI

The man most likely to score points for the Georgians insisted that he, for one, would not be in awe of anyone. 'For me to be playing against Jonny Wilkinson is a great pleasure,' said Paliko Jimsheladze, a former talented wrestling prospect who took up rugby at sixteen partly because a civil war put an end to his wrestling club. 'At the end I hope he will swap jerseys, but I am not afraid of facing him. Why do people say this game is impossible for us? When we go out on to the field we never think about losing. Sure, there is a big difference between us, but I will do everything I can to make this match a spectacle. Maybe it will be not enough, but I tell you this: I have given up a lot for this opportunity and I am ready.'

He was, and so were his team-mates, but come Sunday night, after a day of unseasonal torrential rain after a week of sweltering temperatures, the imbalance between the two teams would tell. While South Africa had put 72 points past Uruguay the day before, England went 12 points better against opponents who fought and defended bravely right to the very end.

In virtually every way it proved to be the perfect workout for England. Scoring twelve tries, conceding none, edging ahead of South Africa in the table after one game, and posting the highest score so far in the World Cup,

England had to work hard for their points, despite what the scoreline suggests. This is precisely what they were looking for, not a romp against hapless opposition. And, although there were concerns afterwards about injuries to all three scrum-halves – Bracken felt a spasm in his back in the warm-up and withdrew, Dawson came off towards the end of the first half and Andy Gomarsall finished the game limping – as well as to Richard Hill and Mike Tindall, at least all twenty-two players in the first squad were given a good run-out. This, in keeping with Woodward's pledge to use every one of his players during the World Cup, was good news.

Woodward and his management team were full of praise for Georgia afterwards. 'The pleasing thing for me was that we had to work for what we got,' said Andy Robinson, 'There weren't any easy scores.' That was true, as the match statistics proved. Under normal circumstances, a tackle count for either side, winning or losing, would be between ninety and a hundred. Georgia had attempted 194 and were successful in 154. Far from collapsing in the face of England's possession and massive territorial advantage, the Georgian novices held their defensive shape, and their blindside flanker, Grigol Labadze, in particular, had an exceptional game.

Pablo de Luca, the Argentinian referee, played his part too, by showing a great deal of common sense during the game. Although the Georgians were repeatedly offside, he warned them against the frequent infringements rather than brandishing yellow cards which would have made life impossible for the underdogs. Never having been involved in a match against such high-calibre opponents, Georgia's failings were those of inexperience and enthusiasm rather than malicious intent.

Predictably it fell to Jonny Wilkinson to score England's first points of this World Cup: he made a far from easy penalty look simple. Although the conditions meant a wet and slippery ball, England had already declared their hand by working their way through half a dozen phases before Georgia were even allowed a touch of the ball. Still, when the Georgian wing Malkhaz Urjukashvili equalised with a penalty (a parity that lasted all of five minutes), even the large contingent of English supporters showed their delight.

Mike Tindall had the honour of scoring England's first try in the World Cup, the centre benefiting from Ben Kay's take of a Georgian throw to the line-out and good linking work by Neil Back to touch down in the 15th minute. Tindall, seen by many as England's most improved player of the past twelve months, yet again demonstrated both his strength and his increased awareness of the try line to score. Wilkinson converted.

Five minutes later, Matt Dawson scored a trademark try when sniping diagonally to the posts from a scrum. Wilkinson converted with ease. Three out of three, and the England stand-off would ultimately succeed with all seven of his pots at goal, two penalties and five conversions, before he was sensibly withdrawn from the fray shortly after the interval. Having given Wilkinson the chance to shake off the cobwebs, there was no point exposing him to possible injury with South Africa just six days away. Besides, in Paul Grayson, England had another world-class number ten waiting in the wings.

By the time Grayson scampered on to the pitch, the game had long been won. Three minutes after Dawson's try, his club colleague Steve Thompson sprinted twenty metres to touch down from a ruck after Kay and Back had done much of the spadework. Then, in the 27th minute, Back himself capitalised when George Chkhaidze lost possession over his own line and right underneath the posts. As the ball lay invitingly across the Georgian try line, Back was the first to arrive to score. This fourth try gave England a bonus point, in addition to the four points for a win, in the revolutionary new scoring system being tested in the pool matches.

If the first half had been hard, the second must have been doubly so for the brave but tiring Georgians. And England indeed scored double the number of tries they'd notched up in the first half. Their first after the break would have demoralised any opposing team. The England forwards shunted Georgia's squat pack backwards at a five-metre scrum five minutes into the half. After the unstoppable surge, Dallaglio joyously dived over the line for a classic number eight's pushover try.

Now the floodgates opened. Seven minutes later, Will Greenwood secured his first try of the match by cleverly vaulting over Georgia's last line of defence and into the corner. Then the Harlequins centre made a telling break, opened up the opposition backs, and fed the grateful Mark Regan, who dived over the line. Regan had been on the field for only fifteen minutes, having replaced Thompson for the second half.

Ben Cohen had not yet featured in the scoring, which was a surprise, considering his voracious appetite for tries. He subsequently scored twice in four minutes. His first bore all the hallmarks of a training-pitch move in Northampton: a perfectly weighted cross-field punt from Grayson, hanging and diagonal, fell into the waiting hands of the England winger, who had nobody left to beat to the line. He had to work a little harder for his second. A forceful run from Lewsey, who was acting as a permanent appendage to the backs line, set up Cohen. A shuffle and a quick step that belied the big winger's size then bamboozled his opponent to allow him to touch down.

Greenwood and Cohen have a competition going among themselves to see who will end up with the most international tries. Greenwood was ahead (he has played many more times for England, though), but the younger Cohen was catching up fast. Still, against Georgia, the increasingly influential centre would have the final say, for now. Darting and weaving his way through a scattered defence, Greenwood dived over the line while a Georgian made a last-ditch tackle. The defender might not have got to the ball, but he certainly inflicted some damage on Greenwood's, if the grimace on the scorer's face was any guide. As he jogged gingerly back upfield, the England man sneaked a quick look down his shorts before making a reassuring two-fingered salute to the crowd. All seemed to be present and correct, thankfully. 'I've never had so many text messages after I've done something than I did after that,' Greenwood admitted later. 'Even my wife got in on the act. She said I should have stuck three fingers up, but she's always been smarter than me.'

Jason Robinson finally got in on the scoring in the final minute. The wing had been well marshalled throughout the game, and while he hadn't done much damage himself, the attention paid to him by the Georgians had created space for others to exploit. The Sale Shark then took his only chance of the game with aplomb. Finally, Dan Luger, who had replaced Tindall just before the break, joined the party, touching down four minutes into injury-time from close range after good support from Lewis Moody, who had come on for Hill.

In the midst of all this, Jason Leonard entered the fray, first to replace Trevor Woodman for a couple of minutes, and then for Phil Vickery permanently with half an hour still to go. In the process, he moved on to 112 test appearances (including the five Lions caps), and broke French centre Philippe Sella's world record. It was an incredible achievement for any rugby player, but all the more remarkable as it was done as a prop – the toughest position on the pitch in terms of the punishment the body has to take.

'We did the best we could,' said Georgia's coach, Claude Saurel.

Indeed they did. 'Georgia kept on tackling right to the very end,' said an impressed Greenwood afterwards. 'There weren't any easy yards out there.' Martin Johnson concurred: 'It was hard work in the mauls and the scrums,' he said. 'There were some big tackles coming in as well. We know that we've been in a tough game, despite the scoreline. We managed to lay down a few markers.'

They certainly did, which was crucial, as a hungry Springbok team had to be faced in just six days' time.

Chapter 6

ENGLAND   25–6   SOUTH AFRICA

Saturday 18 October
at the Subiaco Oval, Perth

England: Lewsey, Robinson, Tindall (Luger, 71), Greenwood, Cohen, Wilkinson, Bracken, Woodman (Leonard, 74), Thompson, Vickery, Johnson (Captain), Kay, Moody, Back, Dallaglio

Try: Greenwood
Con: Wilkinson
Pens: Wilkinson 4
Drop Goals: Wilkinson 2

South Africa: van der Westhuyzen, Willemse, Muller, Barry, Delport, Koen (Hougaard, 69), van der Westhuizen, Bezuidenhoudt, Coetzee (Smit, 60), Bands (Sephaka, 69), Botha, Matfield, Krige (Captain), van Niekerk, Smith

Pens: Koen 2

Referee: P. Marshall, Australia

Attendance: 49,922

MATCH STATISTICS
Scrums Won: England 14 from 15, SA 5 from 7
Line-outs Won: England 11 from 11, SA 20 from 25
Rucks/Mauls Won: England 75 from 78, SA 57 from 68
Tackles Won (Attempted): England 84 (99), SA 100 (117)

While the good news was that England had been given a thoroughly good workout by the determined Georgians, the bad news was the injury count. This would dominate the six days leading up to the most important game in English rugby for four years. Nobody expected a repeat of the teams' previous meeting, when the Springboks had imploded at Twickenham. This time it would be different, and England felt sure that they needed their very best fifteen out there on the Subiaco Oval to quell the inevitable Springbok backlash. In the week before the South Africa match, the Georgian run-out first seemed to have robbed England of some of their stars, then everything appeared to be fine, before finally a few casualties had to be accepted.

Immediately after the Georgia game, therefore, the mood was rather mixed. Kyran Bracken's ongoing back problem had reared up again after he had felt a spasm in warm-up; Matt Dawson had been replaced thirty-eight minutes into the match after receiving a heavy bang to his left leg; and Andy Gomarsall had ended the game with a limp from a bruised shin. Needless to say, the position of scrum-half, in which England had seemed to possess a surplus of talent, was suddenly a cause for concern.

Shortly after the game, head coach Clive Woodward revealed that he had asked Martyn Wood, the in-form Bath scrum-half, to fly out to Perth as a precautionary measure. 'We will monitor the progress made by Matt and Kyran before making any final decisions, up to and including Thursday,' said Woodward. 'We had to make a quick decision to get Martyn on the first plane out here because of jet lag and safety reasons. I am sure Bath will be delighted for him to get his chance. He made a big call to leave Wasps to go there this season, he is clearly playing well and we are lucky to have him.'

Austin Healey should have been the next in line, of course, but he had failed to make the starting line-up for Leicester at the weekend after aggravating a calf strain. Woodward spoke to the utility back but ruled him out as a possible replacement. 'He was devastated,' said Woodward, 'as he would have come out next as scrum-half. He was very honest about his injury and I appreciate that from Austin, who admitted he would be only fifty–fifty for this weekend.'

Within twenty-four hours the injury crisis had deepened. Mike Tindall had limped off against Georgia, while Richard Hill, who had seen out nearly an hour, was nevertheless suffering with a pulled hamstring. Meanwhile, Danny Grewcock was confirmed as having a broken toe, which had come courtesy of an inadvertent stamp from Ben Cohen. Grewcock had been holding a tackle bag during warm-up when Cohen's foot had gone astray, causing a hairline fracture.

By the time a weary Wood arrived in Perth, Dawson's chances were rated as 'fifty–fifty at best', while Bracken, although expected to be back in training within a day, had raised fears concerning his long-term fitness. The deadline for the England team to be named for the South Africa game was 8 p.m. on Thursday night, so the English medical staff were required to work overtime to get as many players fit as possible. Tindall's bruised knee was expected to be fine by the Friday, but Hill's 'minor' left hamstring strain was not responding to treatment as had been expected. The withdrawal of Hill midway during the 2001 Lions' tour of Australia was recognised as a major factor in that team's demise, so England's anxiety was understandable. Since becoming a fixture in the England team back in 1997, injury had barely touched Hill when his country had needed him, but now he, too, was rated as no better than fifty–fifty.

By the Tuesday, although he wouldn't have known it then, Martyn Wood was already about halfway through what must rank as one of the more peculiar periods of his life. As he was not officially a squad member, he was forbidden under tournament rules from staying in the players' hotel, from training with them, even from eating or socialising with them. He was, effectively, under quarantine, waiting to hear whether he would be required. If Bracken was passed fit, Wood would be on the return flight home on Thursday. By Wednesday night this was looking likely. Woodward revealed that he expected, after all, to field his first-choice fifteen for South Africa, with Dawson starting and Bracken fit on the bench. He also indicated that Tindall and Hill should make the grade. For poor Martyn Wood, this meant that he enjoyed all of sixty hours Down Under. Good for air miles, but bad for jet lag. 'It's been a bit surreal,' said Wood. 'I felt a bit like a rabid dog in quarantine. It wasn't as if I was just sitting in my room knocking my head against the walls, but I did get a bit bored. I pretty much knew as soon as I got there that I wouldn't be involved. England never gave me a false sense of hope. They were pretty honest with me from day one. I'm glad I've done it, though. If someone says you've got a chance of joining the World Cup squad, you're going to jump at it, aren't you?'

> **'It's been a bit surreal, I felt a bit like a rabid dog in quarantine.'**
>
> *MARTYN WOOD on his sixty hours Down Under*

Both Dawson and Bracken had wondered whether they, too, might be heading for the Perth departures lounge. 'It's been a tough few days,' admitted Dawson. 'All sorts of things go through your mind. The way it felt on Monday there was no way I was going to make it. I'm a bit surprised I've recovered so quickly.' He was particularly looking forward to pitting his wits against the Springbok scrum-half, Joost van der Westhuizen: 'I always get a buzz when I come up against one of the world's best. He's a huge, huge danger – by far the best scrum-half I've ever seen in a South African jersey. In certain types of games I'd say that Joost is the best I've ever played against. He can be devastating.'

Bracken's fears had been even greater. 'It's been really hard,' he said. 'It brought back bad memories. I've had four years of a pain-free back and then, come World Cup time, I'm struck down twice with it.' (He was forced off with a similar problem during the warm-up victory over France.) 'The problem can be traced back to the old injury, though it's nowhere near as bad. It's just the sort of thing that can flare up. Perhaps it's the hard ground. I was devastated on Sunday night, thinking the worst, in that I might be on the plane home. It took my wife to insist I stayed on and stuck it out.'

Naming his team in the belief that Dawson, Tindall and Hill would all be fit for Saturday, Woodward's squad changes were all on the bench: Martin Corry came in for Grewcock; Dorian West replaced Mark Regan as back-up hooker; and Dan Luger was preferred to Iain Balshaw, who lacked match practice after missing the Georgia game with a calf strain. For Woodward, it had been a busy few days. 'We have a world-class medical team here working up to twenty hours a day on whatever treatment the players require,' he explained. 'We're taking no risks. I trust the medical opinion totally to make the right calls. We got Martyn here for all the right reasons. He's clocked up some air miles but I'd do it all over again with the information I had at the weekend.'

Now both the players and the management team were prepared to start talking about their forthcoming opponents. 'We feel that we can go up a notch yet and we'll have to do so as well,' admitted Lawrence Dallaglio, relishing another crack at the team against whom he had made his international debut eight years previously. 'South Africa are the most physical of the sides we face. There won't be any change on that front. I've always found it a very enjoyable fixture. There's never any quarter given or asked.'

> 'South Africa are the most physical of the sides we face. I've always found it a very enjoyable fixture.'
>
> *LAWRENCE DALLAGLIO*

The big number eight certainly had no fears when it came to Jonny Wilkinson looking after himself, despite the late hit by Jannes Labuschagne that had injured the England stand-off's shoulder and caused the Springbok to be sent off. 'The way that Jonny tackles means that he has the best form of protection any outside-half could want,' Dallaglio explained. 'Trying to get legally to the number ten is a key part of the game, and Jonny understands that and knows what he has to do to have an effect on the game.'

Wilkinson himself said, 'I don't have any concerns about cheap shots in this match and I believe both teams are keen to play rugby. Incidents like the shoulder injury don't carry over into this match. It doesn't work that way. Both teams have moved on and just because it happened in that autumn match, doesn't mean it will occur again. The Springboks are going to be hugely difficult to beat and both teams know that they have to win this match to stay at the top of the pool.'

Besides, Dallaglio felt that South Africa, and especially their captain Corne Krige, had learned their lesson from last time: 'Krige was frustrated at Twickenham because he was leading a tour that wasn't going particularly well, and by the time they faced us they were a fairly depleted squad and had lost to Scotland. It looks like there will be only two survivors in the team we will face on Saturday from that we beat last year, so we already know it is going to be very different. Self-discipline is something we talk about a lot, and while we want to be physical and tough, we have to stay within the laws, and our management make us very aware of this. We have definitely got confidence and momentum coming into this World Cup, but we also know that if we are not physical and play tough then we won't win this match. We have been in some good and bad situations since the 1999 World Cup that have given the team strength, and we are going to need all of that to come through this match.'

Despite the three World Cup warm-up games, plus the small matter of Georgia the week before, assistant coach Andy Robinson admitted that South Africa had been the focus for England for quite some time. 'The real planning for this game took place as soon as the Tri Nations ended,' he said. 'South Africa have been in our minds since then.'

Clive Woodward appeared to be excited by the upcoming clash. 'South Africa have got a very strong team,' he insisted. 'I think they are well prepared. It is a great match-up between two great rugby nations and that's what the World Cup should be all about. We've had a chequered week, but we're used to this. We're an experienced group of players now.'

South Africa's team, as predicted by Dallaglio, contained only two survivors from the Twickenham match: captain Corne Krige and fellow back-row forward Joe van Niekerk would be reacquainting themselves with the English pack. Elsewhere, the Springbok coach, Rudi Straeuli, selected the whole of the Bulls' front five in the hope that the crucial up-front battle would be won by five players who knew one another's game intimately. This meant that prop forward Lawrence Sephaka, who had played in the previous week's thrashing of Uruguay, would be dropped to the bench in favour of Christo Bezuidenhoudt. 'To topple the best team in the world, these guys are going to have to be at their very best,' Straeuli declared.

Compared to England, with the exceptions of Krige and van der

Westhuizen, South Africa were a novice side. Remove those two senior players and the remaining thirteen in the starting line-up averaged no more than ten caps each. Set this against the aggregate total of 580 caps in the England fifteen and the gulf in international experience was clear.

Vice-captain van der Westhuizen, picked for the eleventh time against England, spoke of his determination and confidence. He could have been accused of unjustified optimism in the wake of South Africa's disastrous preparation for the World Cup, during which a racial row had appeared to split the camp. 'We are a united team and we aim to prove a point,' insisted the scrum-half. 'I have a feeling in my heart that we can win. I know exactly what's going on in the camp. There's no racism, no prejudice, nothing like that. I have trained with these guys for the past six months. It's so sad when old players criticise us. "Once a Springbok" should mean "Always a Springbok". As for England, this could be the toughest test of all. But we're not even thinking of losing.'

The fact that van der Westhuizen was still such a major figure in the side was an achievement in itself. In 2002 he had been left out of a Springbok squad for the first time in ten years, a selection decision that had suggested his international career was over. 'That's what I thought, too,' confirmed the thirty-two-year-old, two days before he was due to win his eighty-seventh cap. 'I'm now back to being the scrum-half I was in 1995. I wanted to end my career as I started it, by being creative and sharp.'

His captain then tackled head on the issue of the violence perpetrated by his side in the previous meeting between the two teams. 'When you are in a situation like we were you've got one or two decisions to make,' Krige explained. 'You can either say: "We're getting a hiding, I might as well give up," or you can say: "I'm going down but I'm taking a few guys with me." It wasn't the right attitude to take and I apologised to the people I needed to, and since then I haven't played like that again. As a South African and a Springbok, losing by that margin is totally unacceptable. It took a long time for me to recover from that.'

But recover he had done, to the point where, on the eve of the game, he was the embodiment of passion. 'When you play for the Springboks and you have the type of support we have, every test match is almost a life or death matter,' said Krige. 'The players will have fire in their bellies and ice in their brains. We don't have to stoke up the fires. They are already burning. Our difficulties with England in recent years will make this a nice one to win.'

Gideon Sam, the team's black manager, spoke of the importance of rugby and a Springbok win to the nation. 'I can assure you that there will be people dancing in the streets of Soweto if we win,' he claimed. 'There's been a lot of talk about war, but it's all nonsense. Unnecessary dirty play is not acceptable and the penalties are quite heavy. We're looking to play our best rugby.'

England were looking to do the same, although they had a lot less to prove on the dirty play front. 'We've not had a big issue with penalty counts,' said Andy Robinson. 'Self-control is a part of our game.' As further insurance, though, England had enlisted Steve Lander. Having just missed out on selection as one of the competition's officials, Lander was dispensing advice to the squad on where the referees would be drawing the line. 'The work Steve does for us is tremendously important,' conceded Phil Larder, the England defensive coach. 'His work at full-contact sessions has been essential. I'm sure his presence has made a massive difference.'

> 'As a South African and a Springbok, losing by that margin is totally unacceptable. It took a long time for me to recover from that.'
>
> *CORNE KRIGE on the previous meeting between the teams*

The day before the game, England, rather predictably, were on the receiving end of global criticism. This time it was initiated by John Eales, the former Wallabies captain, who suggested that the English were using illegal tactics in their execution of the rolling maul. If Eales was merely trying to start a debate, the current Australian coach, Eddie Jones, saw this as a heaven-sent opportunity to join in. 'You'd have to say that Eales has a point,' said Jones, ingenuously. 'His comments are very insightful. Little things come into the game and if they're not picked up on, then they become a bigger problem.'

Eales's main comment was directed at the way England use Neil Back at the rear of the maul, with a clutch of forwards in front of him to protect the ball. 'Effectively, what he is doing is being shepherded,' Eales argued. 'It's certainly the equivalent of obstruction and it's the equivalent of a decoy play in the back line. It's exactly the same, except that it's in close. The referee should be giving a penalty because it is clearly obstruction.'

On hearing this, Rudi Straeuli made it known that he would be raising the issue with the match referee, Peter Marshall. 'We'll be dealing with a lot of issues when I meet him,' Straeuli revealed. 'The maul is quite a strong weapon of England's, and Back scores a lot of tries there, both for England and for Leicester. John Eales is, after all, a very astute man who knows his rugby.'

Even Georgia, who, let it be remembered, conceded 84 points to England the week before, joined in the general England-baiting. 'I didn't feel England were as confident as some people said they would be,' announced their French coach, Claude Saurel. 'Even against us they seemed at times to have doubts over their game and to be over-careful about every move. I think that they are so much under stress that they are going to be scared stiff before every game.'

Having grown used to this sort of pre-match psychology, England's response, courtesy of Neil Back, was succinct: 'It's comment borne out of fear,' he said dismissively. Captain Johnson, however, was happy to admit to nerves before such an enormous game. 'We have had a very intense four years since losing the 1999 World Cup quarter-final to South Africa,' he said. 'Everything has moved on: our preparation, fitness levels, test experience as a squad. By hard work we have become very difficult to beat. There have been some notable high points, such as beating South Africa in Bloem-fontein, France in Paris, Ireland in Dublin, New Zealand in Wellington and Australia in Melbourne. But none of these games was as big or as important to England as our next game. It's absolutely massive for both countries. We feel more anxiety about it, more pressure, more nerves than usual, and that is a good sign, because we are about to face the most physical side in the game, a nation which prides itself on its strength and aggression.'

Johnson, at thirty-three, was preparing to face the Boks for the twelfth time, including three as the Lions' captain in 1997. So he knew more about the opposition than anyone. 'Our games against them have usually been tight affairs,' he admitted. 'Overall, I have found them to be a very direct side, big hitters in the tackle and great at offloading passes while in a tackle. Recently they have played a wider game during their warm-up tests, but we all know where Springbok strengths lie. So the battle of the front fives will be absolutely crucial in the tight. It's not rocket science. I want us to pressurise them at the breakdown and get our game on to the front foot early.

'A so-called bad Springbok team is only relative because, like New Zealand, they are historically the giants of world rugby. They have lost only one World Cup game in the three tournaments they have been allowed to enter, including this one. That is the calibre of what we face on Saturday. And both camps are realistic enough to accept that it will be pretty difficult for the losers of this game to go on and win the World Cup.'

Johnson, with his combination of skill and experience, was of course a vital component in Clive Woodward's team. 'Martin is the best lock forward in the world, bar none,' claimed the head coach. 'He is a tremendous man and leader, but people sometimes forget that Johnno is more than just a towering presence on the field. He is a world-class player, totally outstand-ing in all that he does. His captaincy is also fantastic, and what everybody likes about him is that he does not talk a great deal, but when he does every-one shuts up and listens. Having said that, he has probably spoken more this week than I have ever heard from him, because he knows how important the game is. You just know that, either behind the scenes or on the field, he is saying all the right things to the players, and that is a massive plus for a coach.'

Twenty-four hours before the kick-off, England's management was rocked by an unwelcome realisation. Mike Tindall was still on course to make the starting line-up, but the other two members of the first fifteen who had been struggling for fitness – scrum-half Matt Dawson and flanker Richard Hill – were both finally, definitively, ruled out of the match. Dawson would be replaced by Kyran Bracken, whose own back injury was still causing concern; while Lewis Moody came in for Hill, the man often considered to be the heartbeat of the England team. 'There is no difference in quality,' insisted Woodward, trying not to sound downbeat. 'Lewis and Kyran will step up to the plate.' Meanwhile, Joe Worsley and Andy Gomarsall would move on to the substitutes' bench.

'We trained in the morning and the two players weren't quite right,' added Woodward. 'It was a no-brainer. This is not a game in which you want to take any risks. Having to make the changes has not been disruptive. We did all our heavy preparation for this game during the build-up to the Georgia match. The players coming in are very experienced. This sort of thing happens at a World Cup.'

Dawson was obviously disappointed, but also philosophical. 'When I failed the fitness test it was a crushing disappointment, but Kyran will step up to the mark superbly,' he said. 'We are old mates and muckers. He'll be disappointed for me, just as I'll be rooting for him for the whole eighty minutes.'

And so, on Saturday evening, to the long-awaited game itself. The bare statistics suggest that England came through comfortably. They scored the game's only try; Jonny Wilkinson dropped two goals and saw all of his place-kicks sail through the uprights; and the winning margin of 19 points, against one of the world's elite teams, looked impressive. Yet this was anything but the stroll in the park that those facts implied. Indeed, on England's own admission, this was one of their poorer performances for some time. They were end-lessly hassled and aggravated by a fierce and passionate onslaught from the Springboks. While Wilkinson scored with every attempt he made on goal, his opposite number Louis Koen missed four penalties, and England only made it over the Springboks' line because of a slightly fortuitous charge-down of a Koen clearance. So, if the Springbok

> 'We are old mates and muckers. He'll be disappointed for me, just as I'll be rooting for him for the whole eighty minutes.'
>
> *MATT DAWSON on KYRAN BRACKEN*

stand-off had been on-song and Wilkinson had been less than perfect in his place-kicking, the South Africans might well have won. It was that close.

England clearly missed Hill, while Bracken seemed to be somewhat inhibited because of his back. The result was a number of uncharacteristic unforced errors in and around the English pack, and England were lucky that Koen didn't have on his kicking boots to punish them fully. Nevertheless, a win's a win, and victory in this game virtually guaranteed England an easier route all the way to the World Cup final. Furthermore, the other members of world rugby's big five – New Zealand, Australia and France – would not have been able to escape the alarming conclusion that England had not played well, but had still won . . . against South Africa . . . by 19 points. That was a daunting indicator of England's potential when they *did* put it all together. As a happy bonus, it was a very clean game, as both teams had promised it would be.

... the other members of world rugby's big five ... would not have been able to escape the alarming conclusion that England had not played well, but had still won.

Before the kick-off, the authorities had had to call in an apiarist to disperse 400,000 bees which had suddenly converged on the bench area at the Subiaco Oval. Once they'd been persuaded to leave, it was the Springboks who did much of the swarming for the best part of an hour, although England started the stronger. In front of a watching Prince Harry (sporting an England number-ten jersey), Jonny Wilkinson gave his team a great start with a 4th-minute penalty. On 9 minutes, Mike Tindall nearly touched down in the corner after a sweeping passage of passes. Joe van Niekerk denied him with a crunching tackle that hammered the centre into the corner flag. A couple of minutes later and Tindall was almost over again, this time down the right flank, but he was caught just short of the line.

The South Africans looked like they might be overwhelmed, but soon after they began to settle down. Koen landed his first penalty to draw the scores level after 17 minutes, and England started to make mistakes. The second quarter of the game was crucial because South Africa could well have built a winning foundation if Koen had taken his chances. As it was, he missed four consecutive penalty kicks. Three were awarded for transgressions that are rarely seen by a player in an England jersey these days: a high tackle by Moody, a hand in the ruck by Tindall, an offside by the otherwise impressive Back. While two of the penalties were from long range, they were certainly kickable; and Koen would have been more than a little disappointed to miss the other two. To add insult to injury, Wilkinson then fired England into the lead with his second successful kick, before Koen finally stopped the rot with a penalty just before half-time.

The break came at the right moment for a struggling England. They lacked composure, at the breakdown they were second best, and South Africa were definitely on the front foot. If Koen had made all his kicks, they would have been 12 points up. Even Will Greenwood, normally the most composed figure on the field, had let his concentration slip. After one of Koen's penalty misses the centre had flung the ball to Wilkinson for a drop-out. Unfortunately, he had not touched the ball down first, so he was penalised for a forward pass, gifting the Springboks a scrum five metres from the English line. In this half of missed opportunities, Greenwood was fortunate that the South Africans were unable to capitalise on his mistake.

After a few choice words from Clive Woodward and, in particular, Martin Johnson, England emerged from their changing room for the second half in much better shape. Wilkinson was able to boot England to a 6-point lead with penalties in the 44th and 50th minutes after good work from the pack. Still, however, England's ball retention was not up to scratch, and South Africa sensed that the game was far from over.

It looked as if the Springboks would finally breach the hitherto impregnable England defence when their second-row forward, Bakkies Botha, surged towards the line with only diminutive Jason Robinson to beat. The giant Botha got to within a metre of scoring before Robinson, showing all the defensive instincts of a former rugby league superstar, drove him into touch. Then Jaco van der Westhuyzen, with a two-man overlap outside him, chose to chip the ball forward . . . and out. In a game of so few chances, this was a big one squandered.

The key moment of the match followed soon afterwards when, in the 63rd minute, England scored the game's solitary try. The hapless Koen spent so long setting himself for a regulation kick to touch that Lewis Moody was able to get both hands on the ball in his charge. Will Greenwood spotted where the ball had gone before anyone else knew what had happened: it was a mere twenty metres from the South African try line. Displaying his footballing skills, the centre drilled the ball upfield without a defender anywhere near before falling gratefully on top of it. 'Lewis did well to catch Koen and all I had to do was make sure I didn't mess up,' explained Greenwood later. 'The first touch was Goater-style [a reference to Shaun Goater, the former striker for Greenwood's beloved Manchester City]. I nudged it, and the next thing it hit the back of the net. Fantastic.' On hearing this, Neil Back, whose experience had proved so valuable during the game, muttered: 'I'm glad Will decided to touch the ball down this time.'

> 'Lewis did well to catch Koen and all I had to do was make sure I didn't mess up.'
>
> *WILL GREENWOOD*

Moody explained afterwards that his charge-down of Koen's kick was no lucky accident: 'We'd talked in training about pressurising the kickers, specifically Koen, who we thought might be worth pursuing. We knew he'd sit back in the pocket and try to kick it off his right foot, and that's exactly what he tried to do. It hit my paws and Shaggy [Greenwood's nickname] was in under the posts.'

Wilkinson's conversion took England out to a 13-point lead, which sealed South Africa's fate. His two late drop goals, after 67 and 75 minutes, were beautifully executed and brought his personal tally for the match to 20 points.

Afterwards, Clive Woodward was content to have secured the win. 'I don't really care about the errors,' he insisted. 'It's a World Cup and we are not here to be pretty or entertaining. By our own standards, how we know we can play, we were nowhere near it. We haven't been at our best, but we won, and, in the end, with something to spare. If we had played to our absolute best and won with that score, then we would have known there's not much more we could do. But with every game that goes by England will grow stronger.

'Everyone was very calm at half-time and we put it right in the second half. We knew we weren't playing well, but there was no panicking or shouting. In the end it was a victory of sheer physicality, sheer guts and sheer determination. If we'd lost, the whole ceiling would have come down.'

Assistant coach Andy Robinson was happy enough, too: 'We didn't play anywhere near to our best, but, from my point of view, that's often the best way. We want the momentum in our performance to build through this tournament and to improve as we play each game.'

If the management was putting a positive spin on the game, England's captain, as usual, could be relied on to speak plainly. 'We are very relieved,' said Johnson. 'There's been a lot of pressure on this team this week. It was a huge, huge game and we handled it pretty well. It was a tough game and it could have gone differently if they'd kicked their goals in the first half. But the boys responded brilliantly well. In the first half, especially in the first twenty minutes, we fumbled and bumbled and couldn't get out of our half. But in the second half we played a lot better. Jonny Wilkinson was once again fantastic. His drop goals in the second half kept us away from South Africa on the scoreboard. The charge-down try proved to be massive.'

His team-mates by and large shared Johnson's view. 'We lost a lot of ball, we seldom imposed our game-plan and we did not take the game by the scruff of the neck as we usually do,' admitted Ben Cohen. 'Maybe, after all the success we've had, it's easy for people to assume that England are bound to dominate, no matter what the opposition. In a perverse way it could be useful to have produced such a performance. Now we know we absolutely have to improve.'

Cohen's Northampton colleague Steve Thompson was happy to have got the Boks out of the way. 'It was quiet when we got back into the changing room because we knew we hadn't played as well as we can, but there was so much on this game that the result was enough,' he said. 'It was very, very physical up front, especially around the sides of rucks and mauls. We had anticipated the ferocity of the Springbok attack, but feeling it in the flesh was a different matter. Still, although it might have looked from the sidelines that we were in trouble, it never felt like that on the pitch.'

Kyran Bracken was relieved about more than just the score. 'The lowest point for me was going into the match not knowing whether I would last,' he said. 'I was very worried about it, but once I got through the first fifteen minutes I knew my back would hold up. I've played in some big matches, but none of them beats this. To have come through was a defining experience for the team and for me.'

South Africa's captain, Corne Krige, revealed that he'd been encouraged at one point by uncharacteristic dissent in the English ranks: 'I heard the England players shouting and swearing at each other, and I was very happy,' he said. 'I knew we could frustrate them, but it was a game of chess out there and they took their opportunities. At times it can be a cruel sport, because 25–6 looks a terrible score for us. Maybe we have managed to create a little bit of doubt in England's minds and so have given other teams hope. But England proved that, under difficult circumstances, they can still take the points.'

Rudi Straeuli was left wondering whether a golden opportunity had just been lost. 'We should have been up at half-time and I don't think the final score was a true reflection of the game,' said the coach. 'Maybe it was the difference between experience and youth. And, of course, Jonny's kicking.'

By his own admission, Wilkinson had actually produced nothing approaching his best: to the general astonishment of the crowd, his kicking to touch had been, at times, woeful. However, typically and crucially, he'd not missed when there

> 'We want the momentum in our performance to build through this tournament and to improve as we play each game.'
>
> *ANDY ROBINSON*

were points at stake. 'Before the game we would have taken that win,' he said. 'After the game we're probably a little disappointed at some of the things we did, but when you play against a team like South Africa you can never be truly disappointed deep down with winning. It was a great test for us in every sense, a great indication of where we've got to go and what we've got to work on. We've already done some hard work, and it paid off. Now we have to improve if we want to go further.'

Which is probably not what Samoa wanted to hear as they prepared themselves to face England eight days later.

Chapter 7

ENGLAND 35–22 SAMOA

Sunday 26 October
at the Docklands Stadium, Melbourne

England: Robinson, Balshaw, Abbott (Catt, 70), Tindall, Cohen, Wilkinson, Dawson, Leonard, Regan (Thompson, 50), White (Vickery, 50), Johnson (Captain), Kay, Worsley (Moody, 50), Back, Dallaglio

Tries: Back, Balshaw, Vickery, Penalty Try
Cons: Wilkinson 3
Pens: Wilkinson 2
Drop Goal: Wilkinson

Vili, Fa'atau, Fanolua (Rasmussen, 47), Lima, Tagicakibau (Feaunati, 77), Va'a, So'oialo (Tyrell, 80), Lealamanu'a, Meredith (Schwalger, 80), Tomuli (Lemalu, 55), Palepoi, Lafaiali'i (Tuiavi'i, 70), Poulos (Viliamu, 66), Fa'asavalu, Sititi (Captain)

Try: Sititi
Con: Va'a
Pens: Va'a 5

Referee: J. Kaplan (South Africa)
Attendance: 50,647

MATCH STATISTICS
Possession: England 54%, Samoa 46%
Territory: England 59%, Samoa 41%
Line-outs Won: England 16 from 17, Samoa 12 from 15
Rucks/Mauls Won: England 93, Samoa 51
Tackles Won (Attempted): England 92 (119), Samoa 131 (165)

When England flew from Perth to Melbourne the morning after their crucial win over South Africa one key player was missing from the group. Overnight it emerged that Will Greenwood, the man who scored the only try in the win against the Springboks, had already left for home to be beside his pregnant wife, Caro. Greenwood had not told the rest of the squad that Caro had been admitted to hospital in London, preferring to keep his own counsel until after the game. The couple had lost a baby son, Freddie, thirteen months earlier following his premature birth at twenty-one weeks.

Before boarding the flight to Melbourne, where England would be facing Samoa the following Sunday evening, England head coach Clive Woodward explained the situation. 'Clearly there is some concern and Caro will be in hospital for the next month or the remainder of the pregnancy,' he said. 'Assuming everything goes well with the baby, Will should be back in a week's time, but that will be his decision.

'Will was outstanding, considering what happened to his first child. This is quite a traumatic thing he is going through and the way he played was unbelievable. Will came to see me at the start of last week to tell me that there had been complications. He knew how big the South African match was and didn't want the team worrying about him. He wanted it kept it to himself. I spoke to him almost on an hourly basis before the match. He wanted to play and Caro wanted him to play, but we had prepared in the knowledge that if there had been any serious bad news he would have been on the first flight home. It has been a tough week for Will and he has handled it brilliantly. He didn't want the rest of the team to get worried about it so we only told them in the changing room after the game. Caro has also been fantastic. All our best wishes are with them both.'

Greenwood, who was thirty-one on the Monday, explained his decision: 'As things stand I am going to have a week at home to spend some time with Caro. It's been tough but she wanted me to stay and play. It was difficult but there was nothing I could have really done anyway. We've been in constant touch.'

Other members of the squad, too, had every right to be distracted by events at home. Martin Corry's wife was expecting their first child, while Jason Leonard's partner was due to give birth to their third that week. Jonny Wilkinson, meanwhile, was told that his eighty-year-old grandmother had passed away the day before the victory against the Springboks. The news had been kept from him, on the wishes of his family, until after the match.

As if this were not enough, Lawrence Dallaglio found himself under the spotlight for the wrong reasons. In the dying minutes of the South Africa game the number eight punched Springbok wing Thinus Delport, striking out in retaliation for a hand in his face. 'I gave him a bit of a slap,' Dallaglio admitted. The cut caused by the 'slap' needed seven stitches, and forced Delport's absence from South Africa's next game, against Georgia, five days later. However, no action had been taken by the match referee, Peter Marshall, and the International Rugby Board's citing commissioner ruled the next day that the incident was closed.

This decision clearly angered the South Africans, who had referred the matter to the commissioner. 'We're very disappointed that nothing has happened over this,' announced the Springbok coach, Rudi Straeuli. 'We've gone through the right channels, put the documentation in, and we're not happy.'

This was just the first in a series of attacks on England over the next couple of days. Buoyed by what he saw as weaknesses in the English team after their hard-fought win over South Africa, George Gregan, the Wallaby captain, insisted: 'English mistakes under pressure show that they are beatable like anyone else.' *The Australian* newspaper headlined its report of England's win 'Is That All You've Got?' and former All Black Stu Wilson, writing in the *Sydney Morning Herald*, had some harsh words for the beleaguered English number eight: 'Lawrence Dallaglio is the most professional cheat I've seen and a few more in the pack aren't far behind as they were trying to bend the rules to breaking point. As players slow down they're more inclined to give away silly penalties as they try to cut corners and England repeatedly looked like stunned mullets in Perth as Peter Marshall, the referee, told them to stop cheating and let the ball go.' Wilson also suggested that Wilkinson 'showed that when the pressure is on he is far from the perfect player around the field'.

England did, however, receive support from two rather unlikely sources. 'For me, England are the best,' said Bernard Laporte, the French coach. 'They have hardly lost for three years. They are the most complete team and far more mature in their rugby. Besides, what won the last World Cup? Defence. Australia had one try scored against them four years ago. Who has the best defence now? England. It is the best part of their game, the second best part of their game and the third.'

> 'They have hardly lost for three years. Who has the best defence now? England.'
>
> *BERNARD LAPORTE*

Even more surprising was an endorsement from Clive Woodward's old adversary, Wallaby coach Eddie Jones. 'I must admit, I find the criticism a little strange,' he said. 'I must have been watching another game. I thought South Africa played better than they have all season and here's England winning the game convincingly. They absorbed the pressure from South Africa and I thought their performance was first class.'

England's players, meanwhile, leapt to the defence of their colleagues. 'We are not cheats and would be giving away more penalties and picking up yellow cards if that was the case,' argued Trevor Woodman. 'We know how to slow opposition ball down and stay within the rules of the game and it's then up to the referee,' added Mike Tindall.

Clive Woodward attempted to diffuse the controversy by keeping his tongue firmly in his cheek. 'I want to thank all these coaches and players for their feedback,' he said. 'It is excellent. We read it all and take it on board. That's why we want to say thanks for all the comments we are getting.'

On a more serious note, the head coach wanted to remind everyone that Samoa would not be pushovers in the next match. Their substantial wins over both Uruguay and Georgia had proved that. 'We've seen the Samoans play, they are top of the group, and if we turn over ball as we did to South Africa, we'll be punished,' said Woodward. 'It's going to be a pretty tense week. We are going to make one or two changes and I promise you there'll be no complacency.'

True to his word, the next day Woodward named a strong-looking starting fifteen that boasted Martin Johnson, Ben Kay, Lawrence Dallaglio and Neil Back in the pack, and Jonny Wilkinson, Ben Cohen, Mike Tindall and Jason Robinson in the backs. The team also showed seven changes from the side that had started against South Africa, with Robinson moving to full-back to accommodate Iain Balshaw on the wing, Stuart Abbott moving into the centre for the absent Will Greenwood, and Matt Dawson, now back to full fitness, in for Kyran Bracken at scrum-half. In the pack the whole of the front row was changed, with Jason Leonard, Mark Regan and Julian White coming in for Phil Vickery, Steve Thompson and Trevor Woodman. Joe Worsley replaced Lewis Moody in the absence of the still-injured Richard Hill, whose hamstring required a further week's treatment and rest. Martin Corry and Mike Catt were drafted on to the bench as part of Woodward's continuing commitment to use the whole of his thirty-man squad.

To some, the inclusion of the likes of Wilkinson and Johnson raised a few eyebrows. Samoa had a deserved reputation as a team of big hitters, but Woodward felt he needed some of his best players in the mix. 'There's no suspicion of big hits being targeted at anyone in this match,' he said. 'Samoa tackle hard, but so does every side in this competition. We've been impressed with the way they've played and we are putting out a team that is as strong if not stronger than the one against South Africa.' He added, 'The front-row boys have an opportunity to improve our forward power.' And they certainly wouldn't be lacking in experience. The outgoing trio may have boasted 65 caps between them, but their replacements had a total of 153! Second stringers they were not.

For Messrs White and Regan, this was their chance to show Woodward what they could do in a World Cup environment, especially as the England scrum had looked under pressure the previous week against the Springboks. 'I'm delighted to get out there,' admitted tight-head prop Julian White. 'I know there's an element of no-win about it: if we go well people will say that the Samoans don't scrummage, and if we don't the finger really will be pointed. But I'm approaching it like any test. It's my job to make the management think again.'

Mark Regan was similarly eager to make up for lost time. He would be making his first start in the tournament at the venue where, as a non-playing substitute, he had watched his England colleagues record their first win over Australia in Australia the previous June. By his own admission, he had paid dearly for an error of judgement made six years before. 'I came home from the winning Lions tour of South Africa and became my own worst enemy,' he explained. 'I made the mistake of floating around in the glare of my own success, thinking that I'd done it. I lost focus, took my foot off the pedal and it wasn't long before the inevitable happened and I got dropped. They weren't happy with me, and I wasn't happy with myself. I put on a bit of weight, I wasn't as fit as I should have been and I learned the hard way that reputation counts for nothing. This game waits for nobody. It moves on at a pace and, after being part of a successful Lions tour, I didn't move on with it. That cost me two years out of the England squad.'

Having gone from strength to strength since moving from the West Country to Leeds, Regan was now fighting it out with Dorian West for the second hooker's spot behind Steve Thompson. 'Thompson is a great player who will be there for some time,' Regan conceded. 'I knew it would be a monumental effort to make the World Cup thirty, and I have to make sure I make the most of my chance. When I run out against Samoa I'll be bursting with pride because it's the realisation of a dream for me.'

Another relieved player was Iain Balshaw, given the chance to prove himself on the world stage again and buoyed by an endorsement from his head coach. 'This is Iain's big chance,' announced Woodward. 'There is no doubt that he is pushing Josh Lewsey very hard. The back three we have picked here is one of the stand-out back threes in the world. It will be a big night for Balshaw.'

The full-back was relishing the prospect of repaying Woodward's faith in him and rediscovering the form that had made him the star of the 2001 Six Nations. 'When Clive kept picking me for squads when I lost form I felt I was letting him down,' Balshaw admitted. 'I knew I wasn't delivering. I felt a bit of a fool. The key thing is not to try to force it, just let it happen. I've been given my head to play the game as I see it. Being spontaneous is part of my style. It's a big chance for me in a big game. It's my chance to stake my claim to be in the starting fifteen.'

Stuart Abbott, the former South African under-23, had his say, too, on his first start of the tournament, and was quick to point out the probable reason for his selection. 'Proud as I am to get this chance, I feel sorry Will Greenwood has had to return home for personal reasons,' he said. 'I've got big boots to fill in Will's absence but I'm looking forward to it. I've not touched the ground since scoring on my England debut against Wales. I just hope I can do the shirt justice.'

At least reassuring news was filtering back from London concerning the Greenwoods. 'I've been in touch with Will,' revealed Woodward. 'Caro is out of intensive care and things are looking – touch wood – good. We hope to get Will back next Monday or Tuesday after the Samoa game.'

One player who could sympathise more than most with the Greenwoods, of course, was Mike Catt, who had endured such a traumatic time when nearly losing both his wife and his baby daughter the previous year. Now, restored to full health, both Ali and Evie were out in Australia for the World Cup. 'I do hope for the Greenwoods' sake that it's good news from now on,' said Catt. 'Caro would hate to see Will miss this opportunity, but, when you are talking about something like that, a game of rugby is a fairly minor thing. As for me, it's brilliant to have the family here because sometimes it can be pretty boring when you are stuck in a hotel all the time on your own. Clive Woodward has been very open about allowing the family to come over.'

'Caro would hate to see Will miss this opportunity, but, when you are talking about something like that, a game of rugby is a fairly minor thing.'

MIKE CATT

The Samoans, meanwhile, would be employing those two seemingly incompatible components of all South Pacific rugby: fervent Christianity and ferocious tackling. Their forwards' coach was the former All Black back-row legend, Michael Jones, a man who was completely in tune with the Samoan philosophy. With the game taking place on a Sunday, Jones himself would have no direct input in the match because of his long-cherished stance of keeping the Sabbath sacred. His team weren't quite such strict observers, of course, but, nevertheless, 'The boys will go to church before they play,' revealed Jones. 'Our evening prayer meetings and Bible readings are also fundamental parts of our lives. We're a pretty happy-go-lucky people. We don't get over-stressed. We are big believers in the David and Goliath story. We actually believe it's true.

'There is an essence and a spirit that permeates every part of who we are and what we represent,' continued Jones. 'A lot of our values would not flourish so easily in a professional environment. Our team culture is about putting each other first and playing not only for Samoan rugby but for Pacific Island rugby, making a statement that, despite the obstacles, there is a spirit that cannot be quenched. We live out our Samoanism every day. It is a fundamental dimension of what's brought success to the team in the past. It pushes us to fight above our weight. It's the glue that binds us all together: our faith in God and the love of our people. Still, the week running up to the England game has always been the week we've been targeting. If we really want to make a statement at this tournament, then it has to be on Sunday night. We couldn't really have a better window of opportunity.'

Head coach John Boe, the former New Zealand Under-19 coach, concurred, and underlined that the Samoan tackling would be hard but fair. 'We are extremely strong on discipline,' he said. 'These players are now wonderful ambassadors for their country. We always play our Samoan music on the bus. We're happy because we know how much this means to the people in Samoa. This is the game of our lives, and we're having the time of our lives. We face an enormous challenge but the foundation of any upset is belief. And we have belief.'

They also had Brian Lima, known as 'The Chiropractor' because of his habit of rearranging opponents' bones on the rugby field. The thirty-one-year-old centre was playing in his fourth World Cup, and had already scored ten tries in just fourteen games, but it was his fierce tackling that was of most interest to England. 'Samoans are big and hard in the tackle,' Lima explained. 'We pride ourselves on the big hit.' Gloucester's Terry Fanolua, Lima's partner in the centre, reinforced this point. 'I have never seen anyone hit like Brian,' he said. 'He is a real bone-rattler.'

Meanwhile, the Samoans were gleaning advice from Va'aiga Tuigamala. The former winger, when playing rugby league for Wigan, had been the catalyst for Jason Robinson to transform his life and convert to Christianity. Now he was giving his fellow Samoans all the information he had at his disposal to help them stop Robinson. However, he didn't sound too optimistic about their chances. 'Jason is such a freak that you can pitch all your defensive line against him and you know that he will find a way through it,' admitted Tuigamala. 'The best game-plan for stopping him is to put out thirty players and then you might have a chance. He's a shining example to rugby players that size doesn't matter, not if you have a big heart. Stopping Jason is not

'We're a pretty happy-go-lucky people. We don't get over-stressed. We are big believers in the David and Goliath story. We actually believe it's true.'

MICHAEL JONES

going to be an easy task for my countrymen, but to have the opportunity is a rare privilege, not just to play against him, but against the whole England team.'

Two days before the Samoa game, Clive Woodward was prepared to go public about some of his star players. On Neil Back and Lawrence Dallaglio, for example, he stated that both were on trial for their World Cup futures. 'I have left those players out before and I will leave them out in this World Cup if I don't think that they are playing as well as the other guys,' said Woodward. 'It is a huge opportunity for Joe Worsley. This is one of the few times that he has started for England and he is an outstanding player. I am making sure that Dallaglio, Back and Richard Hill, too, understand that with Moody and Worsley around they have to be at their best.'

Worsley certainly understood the importance of the match. 'I need a top, top game to put myself into consideration for the future,' he said. 'I'm excited about it. I've worked my body really hard and I want to see what I can do with it. It is frustrating backing up the world's most experienced back row because international rugby is very addictive and I want to play as much as possible. I am concentrating on this weekend and not a day beyond that. My focus is on bringing everything I can to our defence, which I'll need to because these guys are phenomenal athletes, and an extra dimension to our attack. If I can do that, the management will hopefully take the view that they need me.'

At the helm, once again, would be the steady, towering figure of Martin Johnson. He was determined to remind everyone who was predicting an easy England win that Samoa would provide stern opposition. 'These guys are dangerous,' he insisted. 'If the game loses structure, and we give them enough turnover ball to work with, then eventually they are going to hurt us. They've shown this already in the past three World Cups. They've proved that they are capable of beating the big teams.'

With Jason Leonard breaking yet another record, this time overtaking former All Black Sean Fitzpatrick with the most appearances in the World Cup (eighteen), and Brian Lima setting his own with his fifteenth consecutive World Cup appearance, it promised to be quite a game. And on the night the match not only lived up to expectations, but, for over an hour, looked like it might provide arguably the biggest upset in World Cup history. After 62 minutes of this pulsating game, Earl Va'a, who kicked brilliantly and even gave Jonny Wilkinson something of a lesson in the art of converting, put Samoa into a 20–22 lead with his fifth penalty of the night. It was the third time that Samoa had held the lead, proving that they were not only a force to be reckoned with but a force who refused to lie down.

While England had uttered the usual respectful comments about their opponents in the build-up to the match, even if they'd truly believed what they'd said they must have been astounded by the sheer brilliance of the fierce and determined Samoans on the night. The South Pacific backs were in their customary exhilarating form – great hands, blinding pace and big, bone-crushing hits – but the big surprise was that their forwards matched England's much-vaunted pack for most of the game, not only in the front five but around the fringes of the back row.

However, the match rested on a knife-edge for another reason: England were misfiring again, much as they had against South Africa during the first half in Perth. Although their backs rarely managed to create a free-flowing passage of play, the biggest area of concern was the breakdown in communication between Lawrence Dallaglio, Matt Dawson and Jonny Wilkinson, the three players who form the backbone of the team in their positions at numbers eight, nine and ten. As a result, the lock forwards, Martin Johnson and Ben Kay, played a crucial role in England first hanging on as they faced a ferocious Samoan onslaught and then, after Steve Thompson, Phil Vickery and Lewis Moody had come on early in the second half, pulling away to safety in the final few minutes. If ever England had needed the cavalry to come and save the day, this was it. Fortunately, they obliged.

In the end, England emerged as the victors by four tries to one, claiming a bonus point in the process. They therefore gained certain qualification to the quarter-finals, where, barring a shock defeat to Uruguay, they would be playing a Welsh side who had narrowly beaten Italy the previous day. Yet the result doesn't come close to telling the whole story of a game that Samoa had looked like winning. Perhaps a better indication of what went on in Melbourne is provided by the fact that the usually unflappable Wilkinson missed three kicks at goal, including one from fifteen metres in front of the posts.

The writing had been on the wall early for England. Two minutes in and Va'a kicked a penalty after England were caught offside. Then, in the 4th minute, England conceded their first try of this World Cup, and a contender for the try of this or any other tournament. The Samoan captain, Semo Sititi, was the man who finally touched down, but only at the end of an eleven-phase move involving *forty* pairs of hands. England's defenders were pulled across from wing to wing until Sititi finally eluded Ben Cohen and Jason Robinson to score near the corner. Va'a converted from virtually on the touchline. England were 10 points down and had scarcely touched the ball.

The arrears would remain thus for a further twenty-one minutes until England, realising that they had a game on their hands, reverted to basics. Neil Back scored in the manner he has scored most of his international and club tries. Captain Johnson won a line-out ten metres from the Samoan line and the English pack ploughed on in a rolling maul before Back, hanging on to the back of the forwards, plunged over the line. Wilkinson converted and then, in the 27th minute, slotted home a penalty to draw the scores level.

Everyone assumed that Samoa's fire had been quelled and normal service had been resumed.

Except for the Samoan team, that is, who clearly had not read the script. They were far from finished. Under pressure, England's discipline began to waver again, with first Dallaglio infringing and then Johnson handling in the ruck. Va'a kicked the two penalties to ease Samoa into a 6-point lead.

If the indiscipline was unexpected, Wilkinson's kicking was positively surreal. At 0–10 down he had missed a tough penalty, his first failure in the tournament, which was a big enough surprise. But the kick from fifteen metres that rebounded back off an upright must have had Woodward and the rest of the management team up in the stands scratching their heads in disbelief. The stand-off managed to convert an even easier penalty a minute before the break after Samoa were caught offside, but as the players trooped off back to their dressing rooms, it was Samoa who still held the advantage, 13–16.

> If the indiscipline was unexpected, Wilkinson's kicking was positively surreal.

In the second half Samoa's enthusiasm remained as high as ever, but their effectiveness began to wane, especially after Martin Johnson had taken a grip of his pack and Vickery, Thompson and Moody were introduced. In the 51st minute England were awarded a penalty try by referee Jonathan Kaplan after Samoa conceded a five-metre scrum and then collapsed it as England were driving forward. With Wilkinson's easy conversion in front of the posts, England had finally taken a 4-point lead. Once again, the pundits were predicting that the game was effectively over as a contest.

Once again, Samoa gave them cause to eat their words. Va'a struck back with two more penalties, in the 54th and 62nd minutes, and the rugby world started to believe that the impossible might just happen.

Wilkinson, who had been disappointing up to that stage, was finally stirred into action, though. In the 65th minute he gave England a 1-point lead with a close-range drop goal after a sustained England attack. Then Samoa were finished off courtesy of the stand-off's beautifully weighted cross-field punt five minutes later. The ball sailed over the whole of the Samoan defence and fell into the hands of the sprinting Iain Balshaw, who ran the remaining twenty metres and dived over the line.

Wilkinson clearly hadn't brushed away all of the cobwebs because he missed the conversion, but Phil Vickery sealed the victory six minutes from time by cutting inside two tiring defenders to plunge across the line for his first international try. Mike Catt, who had been introduced into the game only a few minutes earlier, was twice involved in the move, and it was his clever passing from midfield that carved out the gap for the big loose-head prop to exploit. Wilkinson gave himself a confidence boost by slotting the conversion.

After the final whistle the Samoans huddled together to say a prayer before England formed a tunnel to applaud their beaten opponents off the field. England knew they had made hard work of seeing off the South Pacific islanders, and as they braced themselves for a dressing-room inquest Samoa remained on the Melbourne pitch for a full fifteen minutes to revel in their lap of honour.

Clive Woodward tried to remain upbeat. 'I'm pleased,' he announced. 'We know we've got a lot to improve, but I'm totally confident in this team. It's still going to take a good side to beat England.'

His captain was not so positive, however. 'We need to have a look at ourselves and get ourselves sorted out,' said Johnson. 'All the guys are sitting in the dressing room talking about what we need to do to be a better team. We're making too many mistakes. You're not going to beat teams in the knockout stages making that many mistakes, it's as simple as that. You can talk game-plans all day long, but if you haven't got the ball, you're going to struggle to win a game of rugby. When we did have it we turned it over, we lost line-outs and gave away penalties. We didn't touch the ball for the

> **'We need to have a look at ourselves and get ourselves sorted out.'**
>
> *MARTIN JOHNSON*

first fifteen minutes. Not many teams in the world can attack like that. They asked questions of us that haven't been asked for a long time.'

Other players were also prepared to admit that they'd been lacklustre. 'It was definitely a scare,' said Phil Vickery. 'Perhaps we needed that.' Jason Robinson agreed: 'From the kick-off we just weren't on the ball. We went away from what really works for us.' Matt Dawson, too, conceded that England were way below their best: 'You're never going to be happy with conceding as many penalties as we did,' he admitted. 'It would be fair to say as well that in the first twenty-five minutes they were a little bit too good for us.'

Amid all this navel-gazing, though, it took the Samoan coach, John Boe, to remind everyone that England had still won. 'England are as good as I ever thought and are quite capable of winning the World Cup,' he insisted. 'They are a well-drilled side from one to fifteen, and they are very hard to beat.'

Maybe, but Samoa ran them close. Very close. Were Samoa an underrated team who had played to their strengths or were the English joint favourites for the tournament perhaps overrated? Would the match give England the kick up the backside they seemed to need to produce their best or did it reveal that the bigger guns of the Southern Hemisphere need not be afraid of them after all? Time, as always, would soon reveal all.

Chapter 8

ENGLAND 111–13 URUGUAY

Sunday 2 November
at the Suncorp Stadium, Brisbane

England: Lewsey, Balshaw (Robinson, 44), Abbott, Catt, Luger, Grayson (Greenwood, 62), Gomarsall (Bracken, 62), Leonard, West, Vickery (Captain; White, 54), Corry (Johnson, 45), Grewcock, Worsley, Moody, Dallaglio

Tries: Lewsey 5, Balshaw 2, Catt 2, Robinson 2, Gomarsall 2, Moody, Luger, Abbott, Greenwood
Cons: Grayson 11, Catt 2

Uruguay: Menchaca (Caffera, 71), Pastore, D. Aguirre (Captain), De Freitas, Viana (Reyes, 52), S. Aguirre, Campomar, Berruti (Sanchez, 47), Lamelas (Perez, 57), Lemoine (Storace, 70), Bado, Alvarez (Alzueta, 52), Brignoni, Grille (Gutierrez, 57), Capo

Try: Lemoine
Con: Menchaca
Pens: Menchaca 2

Referee: N. Williams (Wales)
Attendance: 46,233

MATCH STATISTICS
Possession: England 66%, Uruguay 34%
Territory: England 66%, Uruguay 34%
Scrums Won/Lost: England 4/0, Uruguay 4/0
Line-outs Won/Lost: England 11/0, Uruguay 11/0
Tackle Success: England 93%, Uruguay 69%

When Will Greenwood arrived back at the England camp the morning after the Samoa game he found his team-mates under attack from all quarters. However, of course, this paled into insignificance when compared with what he had just gone through. 'It was great to see Caro,' he reported. 'It was a real boost for her and for us personally as a family. We spent a lot of time chatting, and life goes on. We learned that when we lost Freddie last September. We're hopeful that in three or four weeks – whenever England go home – Caro will be in a good state. Then, hopefully, the doctors might allow her to come home. She's in hospital for the foreseeable future, but the doctors are doing an amazing job.

'It's important I do what I do to provide for the family's future. Rugby, for me, is almost an escape, something I've done since I was a kid. It's almost comforting to put my kit on and have a game. I wouldn't have come back if I didn't think it was a place that I could get a smile back and look forward to playing my rugby. Of course, it went through my mind that I might not be coming back. I had no idea what I'd be faced with.'

Greenwood was amused to hear how the French had likened his colleagues in the backs to 'diesel cars' after their lacklustre display against Samoa. 'The English backs are powerful runners but, apart from Jason Robinson, they lack speed on the burst,' the French assistant coach, Jacques Brunel, had announced. 'Samoa defended very well and moved forward quickly, cutting off Wilkinson from his outside players. He doesn't like that, as we found out when we beat England in Paris last year.'

On hearing this, Greenwood countered: 'Compared to some of the names we've been called, I'd say that's a compliment. We must be making progress. People are entitled to their opinions, but we'll put on our tin hats and keep on going. We like grinding out victories if it's a case of grinding them out. If people want to liken us to a tractor, or any other form of transport, so be it.'

A far bigger concern after the win over Samoa stemmed from an incident that occurred just before the final whistle. At the centre of the controversy were Dave Reddin, the England fitness manager, and Dan Luger, the replacement wing. With minutes remaining, Mike Tindall was down injured on the pitch receiving treatment. Reddin, also in charge of the reserves' bench, decided to send Luger on to the pitch. In his thirty-four seconds of action, Luger made one tackle and was penalised once, so his contribution to the match as a whole was negligible, but England had still technically broken the rules by fielding sixteen men. In the thirty-fifth second, having been told by his senior touch judge that England were fielding one too many players, the referee, Jonathan Kaplan, ordered Luger off the field.

England stated that the matter was one of procedural misunderstanding on both sides, and sought clarification on the behaviour of one of the officials involved. The Samoans, meanwhile, were not the slightest bit concerned. 'Mistakes do happen and we don't want something like this to blight what was a wonderful game of rugby,' explained their assistant coach, Michael Jones. His head coach, John Boe, agreed. 'We are more than happy,' he said. 'I did notice they had an extra guy out there and I would prefer to play against fifteen rather than sixteen, but there will be no protest.'

Predictably, others were not so forgiving of what they saw as an English indiscretion. The Wallaby coach, Eddie Jones, was quick to make his point. 'This is a serious situation and I hope they are punished,' he announced. 'Their ground official should definitely be censured and reprimanded for not following instructions. We all like to stretch the protocol to the limit and we all like to get players on to the field as quickly as possible. But it's very important that teams follow the protocol because you don't want terrific test matches like England–Samoa spoiled by something as silly as that. England didn't do it by design; it just happened. They should be reprimanded and then let's get on with it.'

The Wallaby number eight Toutai Kefu, who was missing the tournament through injury, went a great deal further than his head coach. 'The bottom line is that rules are rules,' he wrote in the *Sydney Morning Herald*. 'They should be deducted the points they got from the game and the points [should] be handed to Samoa. Luger ran on to the field, he was involved in the play and to suggest nothing should be done is a joke. Even worse, England defied a tournament official. That is the key issue here. Even fining the Poms is only a token punishment. They showed a lack of respect for the tournament official and the whole thing just smacks of arrogance.'

As an investigation was launched, the tournament director, Fraser Neill, called for reports on the incident from several parties: the match commissioner, former Australian captain Geoff Shaw; the fourth official, New Zealand referee Steve Walsh, who was said to have become involved in a heated exchange of views with Reddin on the touchline; the fifth official, Australian referee Brett Bowden; and the England management.

'It was an error, I can assure you,' England head coach Clive Woodward stated categorically. 'I would like to think that if any team made an error like this, there would be an inquiry and no more than that. I don't know how serious this inquiry is going to be.'

When questioned on the barrage of criticism that England seemed to attract each and every week, Woodward, who lived in Australia for five years after finishing his playing career with Leicester, had a clear understanding of the true attitude towards the English. 'I believe that 99.9 per cent of Australians are fantastic people, but there are one or two idiots who ruin it,' he said. 'A lot of friends keep ringing me up out here to say sorry and it's great. It is amusing to hear and read these comments, but they say more about the people making the criticisms than us.'

In the French coach, Woodward once again found an ally. 'I don't know what the punishment should be, but any ruling that would strip England of their victory would be very harsh,' Bernard Laporte said.

A decision was expected on the Tuesday, but it was postponed by twenty-four hours to allow the Rugby World Cup officials to receive all the necessary documentation in relation to the incident. Woodward would be travelling to Sydney to appear at the inquiry. He and the rest of the English contingent were informed that they would be facing two misconduct charges: for having sixteen players on the pitch, thus ignoring match official Brett Bowden's instructions; and for a second complaint against Dave Reddin, who was allegedly involved in a post-match bust-up with Steve Walsh. Irish lawyer Brian McLoughlin would be sitting in judgement at the hearing.

> 'I believe that 99.9 per cent of Australians are fantastic people, but there are one or two idiots who ruin it.'
>
> *CLIVE WOODWARD*

On a happier note, Jason Leonard found out on the same day that he had become a father for the third time, which provided a good excuse for the team to escape the furore and wet the baby's head. 'I'm not a very emotional person, but I am very proud,' said the world's most capped forward. 'Everyone in the squad has said to me: "I hope the girl looks like Mum, not Dad." And, to a man, each thought he was the first to say it. Had there been any unforeseen complications, I would have flown back. But as all was under control I think my going back would have caused more disruption in the house than anything else. It was a decision we both made to keep me over here. It's a weight off my mind, though.'

In the midst of all this, England somehow had to remind themselves that they still had one final pool game on their hands, an interesting encounter with Uruguay in Brisbane that Sunday. Although nobody expected anything other than a substantial England win, Uruguay had covered themselves with glory by comfortably beating Georgia in the basement battle of Pool C on the Tuesday. So, just like the Eastern Europeans had in England's first match, the South Americans could pose a problem or two. With this in mind, the selection of England's starting fifteen for the Uruguay game, announced on the Wednesday, made interesting reading. Andy Gomarsall and Paul Grayson would provide the half-back pairing; Mike Catt and Stuart Abbott were the centres; Iain Balshaw and Dan Luger were on the wings; and Josh Lewsey reverted to full-back. In the pack, Phil Vickery would captain the team, with

Dorian West and Trevor Woodman alongside him in the front row. Danny Grewcock, now recovered from his broken toe, and Martin Corry, who would be arriving back in Australia only on the Friday from a trip back home to be with his heavily pregnant wife, would form an interesting second row. The young pretenders, Joe Worsley and Lewis Moody, were given the nod as flankers, with Richard Hill still suffering from the injury he picked up in the Georgia game.

The decision to include Lawrence Dallaglio at number eight, making the former England captain the only man to start all four pool games, was the key talking point, and not just because Vickery was favoured ahead of him as captain. While continuing to pick Dallaglio, the head coach had not exactly been showering this senior player with praise. 'Lawrence has had a couple of quiet games and we want him to get a bit more involved than he has,' Woodward revealed. 'I think he's a yard off the pace at the moment. I want him to concentrate on his own game, which is why I've gone with Phil as captain. We want Lawrence back playing at his best. He needs a big game this weekend.'

Dallaglio had faced similar criticism when he was initially dropped for the Australia fixture the previous autumn at Twickenham, and again against the French in the Six Nations. 'It's easy to point the finger at me, but we're all a long way from the standards we're aiming for,' Dallaglio responded. 'I know that the onus is on the senior players and I've got the opportunity to give the team a lead on Sunday. I certainly intend to do that. Everyone needs a big game. We all know that. What we're looking for is an eighty-minute performance.'

Woodward's major concern, however, was over the high number of penalties England were conceding: fourteen against South Africa and fifteen against Samoa. 'It's disappointing because we have a single-figure target,' the head coach explained. 'If we are to win the big games coming up, we can't have a penalty count that high. It affects a game massively. We've got to be smart enough within games to cope. There's no point being sorry afterwards about it. We're way out on that part of our game at the moment.'

With the team for the weekend announced, all attention inevitably then turned back towards Sydney. Accompanying Woodward at the disciplinary hearing were the resident England lawyer Richard Smith, Dave Reddin, players Dan Luger and Andy Gomarsall, and the team's director of communications, Richard Prescott. After a four-hour hearing, England were relieved to discover that their indiscretions during the Samoa game would not be too costly. The punishment was a 10,000-pound fine and a two-match touchline ban for Reddin. Given that the worst-case scenario was that England could have been docked some points, the English delegation was relatively happy. The second misconduct charge against Reddin, for his heated exchange with

Steve Walsh, was dismissed by Brian McLoughlin. It emerged that Walsh, who was due to run the line in two days' time in the game between France and the United States, still had to answer a complaint that he had made unsuitable comments to English officials.

'There was a range of mitigating circumstances, including a clean record, character evidence and an apology,' explained McLoughlin, who was keen to draw a line under the whole episode. 'But this was weighed against a number of factors, including the fact that the directions of the match official were ignored and the need to maintain the integrity of the match officials.'

The official English response went as follows: 'The England squad are delighted that this verdict has been reached. Dave Reddin is and will continue to be a valuable and well-respected member of the squad. The England squad and management accept the judgement and now look forward to the fixture against Uruguay on Sunday.'

Shortly afterwards, Steve Walsh received a one-match ban, preventing him from taking up his duties in the France–USA game. His behaviour was labelled 'inappropriate' in a statement from the World Cup officials.

'I hope the IRB hand over the ten thousand pounds to them [Samoa] because I think they deserve it more than any other team I've seen so far.'

CLIVE WOODWARD

Woodward, meanwhile, having returned to the England base at Surfers Paradise, just south of Brisbane on the Gold Coast, revealed a novel idea. He had been so impressed by Samoa, both in the match and in their dignified behaviour in the ensuing sixteen-man controversy, that he suggested the fine should go directly to the South Sea islanders. 'Samoa have been outstanding,' he said. 'They were clearly being put under an immense amount of pressure to say something and they wouldn't have anything to do with it. I hope the IRB hand over the ten thousand pounds to them because I think they deserve it more than any other team I've seen here so far.'

Having been half a world away throughout the controversy, Martin Corry returned, bleary-eyed, to the camp on Friday. Three days earlier he'd witnessed the birth of his first child, Eve. He was training within three hours of landing. 'It was a phenomenal experience and it's difficult to put into words what it was like after Eve was born,' Corry explained. 'I can't thank Clive Woodward enough for all his support. I spoke to him before the World Cup and asked, if I was selected for the final thirty, if he would consider sending me home for the birth of the baby. Clive told me I had his backing. Now Eve has been born and my wife, Tara, is fine I'm completely focusing my mind on the Uruguay match.'

Meanwhile, away from the glare of publicity that surrounded the England camp, Uruguay were preparing for the biggest game of their lives. On the Tuesday night, captain Diego Aguirre had led his men to a historic 24–12 win over Georgia in Sydney. Their reward was an 800-mile flight north to Queensland and the prospect of just four days' recuperation and preparation. They could not even celebrate in style: 'The restaurant closed early so we had to go back to the hotel,' Aguirre, from Montevideo, explained. The centre, like all but three of his team-mates, was not a professional rugby player. A graphic designer by trade, he had closed his business for six weeks, thereby losing a small fortune, to travel to Australia for his adventure of a lifetime. 'I don't know how much this World Cup will cost me, but it doesn't enter my thinking,' he explained. 'My philosophy is that I play the game because I love it. I am proud to wear the shirt of my country. Memories are more important than money.'

The Uruguayans, nicknamed 'Los Teros' after a small, indigenous bird that struggles to fly but which is obdurate and protective, had stirred the imagination of their otherwise football-mad people back home. Indeed, the World Cup games were being broadcast live into Uruguay. 'They may not understand the laws of rugby, but they understand the colour of our shirt,' Aguirre added. 'But my friends still ask me if I am crazy.'

He and his team-mates knew that the game against England would be a new experience for them, a step up even from beating the likes of Canada and the USA in Montevideo to qualify for the competition. 'It will be our toughest ever match, but reputation counts for nothing out on the pitch,' insisted number eight Rodrigo Capo, who had just finished his first professional season with French club Castres. 'What we have in our team is a great spirit. We are all friends and give up time and money to play for Uruguay. It is a beautiful experience.'

Back at the England camp, the players were making final preparations after some time relaxing. Most of the squad had spent an afternoon at the local water park, Wet 'n' Wild. Josh Lewsey takes his watersports more seriously and relished the opportunity to catch up on some surfing, something he enjoys in Cornwall when back home. 'You either let the pressure to keep your place get on top of you or else get on with it and enjoy the experience of having so many good players around you on the pitch,' he said. 'One of the strongest aspects of this squad is the mutual respect. We are winning the games without playing our best rugby and that's a healthy sign. Whenever I have been involved in successful teams it's been when morale is high and everyone is relaxed. This week we have been given time to chill out and enjoy the experience of being part of the World Cup. I have been down to the beach to surf while other guys headed to the golf course. If you didn't have some down time, then you would become stale.'

Danny Grewcock was perhaps in a more serious mood in the build-up to the match. The England lock had been out with his broken toe since the warm-up before the Georgia game. 'I was worried,' he admitted. 'I began to wonder if I'd miss out completely in this World Cup. It was a freak injury, an accident. Although it was bloody sore when it happened, I thought the pain would wear off when I sat on the bench. But it got more painful and an X-ray showed a clean break in the second toe of the right foot. Fortunately it was a "good" break and the medical team told me it was not a big deal.'

While his team-mates had been training, the Bath captain had strength-ened his foot underwater by spending long periods walking up and down the team hotel's swimming pool. 'There is no denying the empty feeling I experienced when I saw the boys celebrating in the dressing room after their wins,' he said. 'That's why I can't wait to get a game under my belt.'

Another player eager to prove a point was Andy Gomarsall, making his first start of the World Cup. 'Clive said to me when I came out here: "I don't just want you to be the number three scrum-half." My immediate answer was to say that I didn't want to be the number three either. Maybe it still does look that way, but I certainly feel I can make the team. I've got the bit between my teeth and I feel sharper than ever. I really want to press the advantage home. I want to say to Clive: "I'm here, I'm ready, I can do it."'

Paul Grayson's reaction to the suggestion that he might lay a claim to the number-ten jersey permanently showed that he hadn't lost touch with reality just by being picked for the Uruguay match. 'What, shift Jonny out of the side within a week?' he asked. 'That might be a slightly tall order. No, for me, it's just great to get another start for England and the chance to be part of another World Cup. For a few of us, there have been months of pain and sweat just to get on the plane.'

Several others in the England team were also not afraid to be realistic. 'We've said as a group that we think we can improve,' admitted Jason Leonard. Iain Balshaw agreed: 'We know we can get better. Everyone knows we've got to pick it up.' Captain for the day Phil Vickery was similarly deter-mined. 'We're by no means playing the way we can,' he said. 'None of us has played particularly well. It's very important that we go out and lay down some markers.'

Which they most certainly did against a brave but outclassed Uruguay. England scored their most points ever in a World Cup match: 111. Their total of tries, seventeen, equalled the team's record for any test match. And, in scoring five tries, Josh Lewsey became only the third Englishman to achieve that feat in over a hundred years of international rugby. Better still, after some hiccups against both South Africa and Samoa, England returned to their 'A' game. This may have been against inferior opponents, but England certainly looked much the better for a week's relaxation and easier training up at Surfers Paradise.

'There is no denying the empty feeling I experienced when I saw the boys celebrating in the dressing room after their wins. That's why I can't wait to get a game under my belt.'

DANNY GREWCOCK

The victory left England comfortable winners of Pool C, with a quarter-final to look forward to against Wales. Although, when watching the epic New Zealand–Wales clash after warming down, the English team for a moment must have thought that they would be facing the All Blacks instead. South Africa finished runners-up in Pool C and would meet the somewhat shell-shocked Kiwis. For brave Samoa, Uruguay and Georgia, the World Cup was over.

On the downside for England, both Iain Balshaw and Danny Grewcock were injured during the demolition of Los Teros, while Joe Worsley took the shine off a good personal performance by high-tackling Joaquin Pastore. Worsley sat out the last three minutes of the match in the sin-bin. As if this were not bad enough, the flanker had bowed and then applauded the crowd as he headed off the pitch. While Worsley was enjoying himself, Pastore was still prostrate on the ground receiving treatment.

Still, the positives far outweighed the negatives. And the match went some way to erasing the memories of England's last visit to the Suncorp Stadium, back in 1998 during the so-called 'Tour of Hell', when a severely under-strength England were thrashed 76–0 by Australia.

For Clive Woodward, the performance provided some welcome selection headaches. Balshaw looked back to his best before a sprained ankle forced his withdrawal early in the second half. And the man Balshaw was challenging most fiercely for a starting place against Wales, Josh Lewsey, had not exactly had a quiet game himself. Stuart Abbott and Mike Catt had formed an exceptional partnership in the centre, Paul Grayson looked every inch a world-class stand-off, and Andy Gomarsall, with two tries and first-rate service to Grayson, advanced his claims over rival scrum-halves Matt Dawson and Kyran Bracken. Up front, Lawrence Dallaglio went some way to answering his head coach's midweek criticisms.

'It was like Formula One running against a bicycle,' admitted Daniel Eduardo, the Uruguay manager. 'It was like a lion against a mouse.'

Indeed it was. Only twice was England's line under any serious threat. Early on (and already behind after Lewis Moody's 3rd-minute try), Uruguay camped inside England's twenty-two for the best part of seven minutes. They were eventually seen off after a Juan Menchaca penalty. Then, in the second half, Pablo Lemoine bulldozed his way over from close range. Unsurprisingly, the small Uruguayan contingent (and virtually every neutral) inside the Suncorp Stadium went wild.

Probably quite a few English fans cheered too, because by then the result was in no doubt whatsoever. Moody's fine touchdown in the corner, a brace from Balshaw, Lewsey's first of the night and one a piece for Catt and Gomarsall had secured a 42–6 half-time lead for England (Menchaca had added a second penalty right on the whistle).

In the second half England sent on the scarcely needed cavalry. Martin Johnson took over from Martin Corry, who had tweaked a hamstring; Jason Robinson replaced Balshaw, who worryingly left on a stretcher; and Will Greenwood came on for Grayson, with Catt moving to stand-off to allow Greenwood to take up his customary position in the centre. The result was devastating. England moved from 50 points to over 100 in barely half an hour.

But while all the talk at half-time had been about how many England would score, this was soon revised to how many Josh Lewsey would score. His second try had come just 53 seconds into the second half, and, while Dan Luger stole some of his thunder with a trademark run down the left wing to score, from then on the star was certainly the full-back. His five tries equalled Dan Lambert's achievement against France in 1907 and Rory Underwood's against Fiji in 1989. 'This is the stuff of boyhood dreams,' Lewsey admitted later. 'The forwards provided the ball and the midfield guys gave us the chance to show what we're capable of. The most important thing was that we needed a decent performance to rebuild confidence for the knockout stages. As for me, I wasn't aware of the record. I didn't even score against Georgia, so it was nice to get on the scoresheet.'

If Lewsey stole the show, though, England's dominance was emphasised by the fact that every back, with the exception of substitute scrum-half Kyran Bracken, scored at least one try. Catt and Gomarsall grabbed another each; Greenwood announced his return from the trials and tribulations of the past ten days with one more to add to his huge international total; and Jason Robinson notched a brace, displaying his blistering pace on the right

But while all the talk at half-time had been about how many England would score, this was soon revised to how many Josh Lewsey would score.

wing. But the pick of the second-half tries came from Stuart Abbott, who bamboozled the Uruguayan defence with two textbook sidesteps that opened up the opposition to allow him to score his second try for England. To cap it all off, Grayson converted eleven from thirteen, a figure even Jonny Wilkinson would have been satisfied with, while Catt struck another two.

Afterwards, however, the quality of England's performance was rather overshadowed by the Joe Worsley incident. Clive Woodward was quick to make it known that he had severely reprimanded the Wasps player. 'It wasn't the brightest thing to do and I've had very serious words with him,' revealed the head coach. 'It was a big, big mistake. I wasn't at all happy with what he did, but he'll learn from it. A rebuke is enough. We all make errors, but I must apologise on his behalf.'

Worsley wasn't prepared to let his boss take all the flak for him, though, and appeared later that night. 'My gesture of applause to the crowd was a misplaced one and an error of judgement,' he admitted. 'I would like to apologise unreservedly to the Uruguay squad and fans and wish them every success in the future.'

The other major cause for concern, certainly for the English press, was Balshaw's injury. Woodward, however, was unperturbed and in joky mood. 'The official line from the doctor is that Iain has a minor ankle strain . . . So he's probably going home tomorrow!' said the head coach, in a reference to the somewhat over-optimistic prognoses he'd been given for English players earlier in the tournament. 'Seriously, we are hoping the injury is not as bad as it looked.'

Woodward continued, 'The phoney war is over and I'm really looking forward to getting on with what we have been focused on – the knockout stages. After we won the South Africa match, everyone relaxed and I became confident that this would be a very good tournament for England. There's a change of mindset now as the real thing begins, and I just believe that this is a big-match team.'

The last word, however, should go to Josh Lewsey. He had been watching from the stands when England had been hammered in Brisbane five years previously. 'If you were English, you hurt that night,' he recalled. 'It's been a long road from there, but in adversity and difficult situations you learn more. Clive and the players learned a great deal from it and it's taken a few years to come to fruition. But now it really has started to bear fruit. As for me equalling Rory Underwood's record, all I can say is that Rory is an absolute legend and it's very nice to be mentioned alongside him.'

Next to try their luck against the English in the Suncorp Stadium would be Wales, runners-up in their group perhaps, but riding on a wave of confidence after their sterling effort against the All Blacks. In the aftermath of that match, and with Australia scraping home by a point against Ireland and the

French looking decidedly ordinary against the USA, England once again seemed worthy favourites for the tournament. But there was no room for complacency. One defeat would mean the end of England's World Cup dream, and if the Welsh had been written off by everyone before the New Zealand match, no one was making the same mistake now.

Chapter 9

ENGLAND 28–17 WALES

Sunday 9 November
at the Suncorp Stadium, Brisbane

England: Robinson, Luger (Catt, 40), Greenwood (Abbott, 53), Tindall, Cohen, Wilkinson, Dawson (Bracken, 68), Leonard (Woodman, 45), Thompson, Vickery, Johnson (Captain), Kay, Moody, Back, Dallaglio

Try: Greenwood
Con: Wilkinson
Pens: Wilkinson 6
Drop Goal: Wilkinson

Wales: G. Thomas, M. Jones, M. Taylor, I. Harris, S. Williams, S. Jones (Sweeney, 59–72), Cooper (Peel, 65), I. Thomas, McBryde (M. Davies, 64), A. Jones (G. Jenkins, 29), Cockbain (Llewellyn, 48), Sidoli, D. Jones, Charvis (Captain), J. Thomas (M. Williams, 58)

Tries: S. Jones, Charvis, M. Williams
Con: Harris

Referee: Alain Rolland, Ireland
Attendance: 45,252

MATCH STATISTICS
Possession: England 63%, Wales 37%
Territory: England 57%, Wales 43%
Tackles Made (Missed): England 105 (30), Wales 174 (28)
Rucks and Mauls: England 126, Wales 62
Ruck and Maul Turnovers: England 4, Wales 11
Line-outs Won: England 11 of 12, Wales 18 of 21

England versus Wales has always been and will always be a huge fixture in its own right, but with the added incentive of a World Cup semi-final place up for grabs this match took on a new dimension. In recent years, and especially in 2003, England had got the better of the Welsh by some distance. Although their Six Nations game in Cardiff had been testing at first, England ultimately came through with relative ease, and when a second-string England played a full-strength Wales again in the Principality during their World Cup warm-up, a record win was posted.

But that was history, especially in light of the Welsh display against New Zealand the previous Sunday, which led all neutrals to believe that this quarter-final suddenly looked very competitive indeed. And if the neutrals thought that, the Welsh themselves were even more optimistic. Shortly after their 53–37 defeat at the hands of the All Blacks, the star of the Welsh show, young flanker Jonathan Thomas, spoke for the rest of his team-mates: 'We've learned a lot from this game and now we believe we can beat England. It's going to take an even bigger effort than the one we've just produced, but we've really come on as a squad and we can definitely win. We've been given fresh belief.'

His captain, Colin Charvis, agreed. 'We feel we have taken a few rungs up the ladder and what we've got to do now is try to improve again,' he said. 'Against England we're going to have to take another two steps up that ladder.'

Even John Mitchell, the New Zealand coach and former assistant to Clive Woodward with England, thought that new spice had been added to the quarter-final. 'The match isn't at Twickenham and Wales can take a lot out of this,' he warned.

Back in the England camp, Danny Grewcock's miserable year took yet another turn for the worse. The punch-up with Lawrence Dallaglio in the Parker Pen Cup Final, his consequent omission from the summer tour and the broken toe sustained in the warm-up against Georgia were now all thankfully behind him, but fate had another trick to play. Having played against Uruguay in England's final pool game, the Bath captain discovered after an X-ray that he had broken his left hand against Los Teros. His World Cup was over.

'On behalf of the squad I'd like to thank Danny for the huge contribution he has made to our Rugby World Cup preparations,' Clive Woodward stated. 'He has retained a really positive attitude throughout the last few weeks and he had an outstanding game against Uruguay.'

As the lock forward returned home, his replacement, Simon Shaw, who had been very unlucky to miss out on Woodward's final thirty selection in the first place, was making his way over to Australia. According to Warren Gatland, the Kiwi coach of Shaw's club Wasps, the giant lock had offered to play against Newcastle in the Zurich Premiership. 'I turned his offer down because I couldn't have lived with myself if Simon had played and picked up an injury,' said Gatland. A weary Shaw arrived at England's Brisbane hotel on the Tuesday morning, having received the call from Woodward on the Sunday. The last time he had taken a call from his head coach it was to learn that he had failed to make the World Cup cut. 'That was a brief conversation,' Shaw admitted. 'There were a couple of four-letter words there and then I put down the phone. I got on with what I was doing that Sunday, which was moving house. I was driving a truck at the time, so it was a good job I didn't suffer road rage. It was a huge blow at a chaotic time, what with a new-born child and moving house. I felt I had done enough in the warm-up games to warrant a place. Then I kind of blanked out the World Cup. It really hit me when the first game was played, then it was a couple of weeks before I started watching the matches. On Sunday there was a message on my phone from Clive. It was the one time that I've rushed to call him back.'

Having missed out on the last two World Cups through injury, Shaw was not going to turn down this opportunity. 'I'm still in a state of shock,' he explained. 'I spent all day Sunday consoling my partner, Jane, who was tearful. It's a huge thing for me to be here at the World Cup. Physically, I couldn't be in better shape, although the so-called recovery session to get over the journey almost killed me. I'm just delighted to be here.'

With Grewcock gone, another injury was still causing great concern. Richard Hill, seen by most as invaluable to England's cause, had played only fifty-two minutes of World Cup rugby against Georgia before injuring his hamstring. What should have been no more than a minor niggle had turned into a major headache, and Woodward was finally prepared to concede that his medical team were struggling to find an answer.

Hill's colleague in the back row, Neil Back, revealed just how much the team missed the number six. 'He is unique,' said Back. 'His work-rate is amazing. I hope he's fit as soon as possible.'

Zinzan Brooke, the former great All Black flanker, was in no doubt that 'England need Hill. I'd go as far as to say that if Richard Hill is not there, then England will not win the World Cup.'

With or without Hill, though, life had to go on, and by the Wednesday before the clash with Wales, Woodward was in a position to announce his squad of twenty-two for the quarter-final. Of most interest was the inclusion of Jason Leonard, who, by receiving the nod from the England management, would unequivocally equal the world record of 111 international caps held by the French centre, Philippe Sella. (Although, as mentioned earlier, Leonard had already sailed past that mark if one includes his five Lions caps

> 'I told Jason when I was in London a few weeks ago that I would be there when he equalled the record, even if it meant going to Australia.'
>
> *PHILIPPE SELLA*

in his total.) In Paris, the legendary Sella, on hearing news of Leonard's selection, was planning to make the 10,200-mile journey down to Brisbane to present the English prop with a bottle of the finest claret. 'I told Jason when I was in London a few weeks ago that I would be there when he equalled the record, even if it meant going to Australia,' Sella explained. 'Now I must be on my way.'

The venerable loose-head prop was his usual modest self in spite of all the fuss, and was genuinely taken aback by Sella's mission. 'It's a long way to come to say hello, but that's Philippe for you,' Leonard said. 'He's quite content for me to call it a day and arrange a big party in his home town, but I don't think I can be bribed.'

Leonard's selection was clearly not down to sentiment, either. He had regained the number-one spot from Trevor Woodman, who, despite fitness doubts, had passed a rigorous test on his suspect back before the squad was announced. The Gloucester prop would be sitting on the bench.

'Jason is in on merit,' explained Clive Woodward. 'For him to get in against so much competition is a tremendous accolade. He's earned every single one of those caps, but this is not about his hundred and eleventh test. It's about England winning.'

Leonard could well recall the last time England and Wales had met in a World Cup quarter-final, back in 1987, when the Welsh prevailed 16–3. 'I watched it on TV and remember it as a bit of a scrappy old game, with Wales deserved winners,' he said. 'It's funny, but only the other day I was trying to recall the Welsh pack that played that day. And then the scary thought struck me that I began playing against them a couple of years later. They had a rerun of the 1991 England versus Australia World Cup final on television the other night and some of the younger players were saying, "Cor blimey, you props had it easy back then. All you did was go from line-out to scrum and back again." It's true that you were never expected to carry the ball in those days or make too many tackles. The game has turned full circle and now everyone is involved in everything. I'd like to see some of those younger fellows going in for a couple of scrums and see if they are still laughing when they come back out.'

When Leonard's international career began over thirteen years ago, in an intimidating Buenos Aires against a fierce Argentinian pack, his fellow prop Jeff Probyn gave him some invaluable advice: 'Treat your first cap as if it's going to be your last and you won't go far wrong.' It's something to which Leonard has adhered ever since, although his professional career could well have ended only two years after that first cap but for some major neck surgery which involved drilling through his windpipe to repair a ruptured disc.

'I'm more surprised than anyone that I'm still going,' admitted Leonard. 'When I started, thirty caps represented an exceptional England career. I remember saying after the last World Cup that I probably wouldn't make it to 2003. I know plenty of people who go to work and have a terrible day at the office. I've got a great job, I play rugby, and the only thing you can be sure of is that I won't be playing in the next World Cup.'

Elsewhere, Lewis Moody would once more be deputising for the injured Richard Hill, and Matt Dawson received the nod at scrum-half ahead of substitute Kyran Bracken, who would claim his fiftieth cap if he came on to the field, and the unlucky Andy Gomarsall, who was left out of the squad. The only other concern centred on Mike Catt, whose position on the bench was dependent on his recovery from a training-ground accident which resulted in him being taken to hospital with a neck injury, although he was later discharged when it turned out not to be as serious as had initially been suspected.

On Thursday the England players broke their silence on the weekend fixture. 'You'll not find a more excited bunch of boys than the English and Welsh squads,' said centre Will Greenwood. 'How good were Wales on Sunday? That was fantastic to watch as a fan, never mind as someone watching a potential opponent. It just shows that any side that gets through to the last eight can have a crack at this thing. We'll have to perform to our very best, and if we're not at our very best, then we'll come a cropper. It's all very positive, though, isn't it? I wouldn't want to be anywhere else in the world right now.'

Josh Lewsey, the five-try hero against Uruguay, was looking forward to continuing his fine form against the Welsh. 'As a team, we were a bit below par against South Africa,' he admitted. 'We went inside our shells a bit, and fell away from the rugby we've produced for the past two years. So last weekend was about playing how we want to and coming off the field with smiles on our faces. If we're honest with ourselves, we knew our attacking game had been slightly below par. So there were two objectives against Uruguay: one was to enjoy it; the second was to apply some patterns we intend to use in the later stages of the

'...Wales are a whole different force, and they showed against New Zealand that they command respect.'

JOSH LEWSEY

103

tournament. It was just nice to get the ball with some time and space. We've been criticised in the past for not being creative, but against Uruguay we showed what we're capable of when we use the ball properly. That said, we're fully aware, with due respect to Uruguay, that Wales are a whole different force, and they showed against New Zealand that they command respect.

As did Lewsey himself from his head coach: 'Ever since he got this chance in the Six Nations against Italy at Twickenham earlier this year he's scored tries for us,' said Woodward. 'He's incredibly powerful, and a little bit more of an orthodox full-back than Jason Robinson. He gets his hands on the ball more than any other full-back I've come across. He has this great ability to support the play. To have Lewsey in there and Balshaw on the bench means we're incredibly lucky.'

Jason Robinson was full of praise for the Welsh. 'I was glued to the television set, watching Wales take the game to the All Blacks,' he said. 'They were playing the type of rugby everybody aspires to. Let's be honest, prior to the World Cup Wales were struggling. Rugby in the Valleys had been at its lowest ebb for many a year, but I always knew Wales had players with the ability to break through. Any side who can score four tries against the All Blacks must be taken seriously. In the recent past the Welsh have lacked confidence, but I saw it oozing out of them last week in that game. They'll have nothing to lose against us, they'll be looking to throw the ball around, and we're going to have to front up early on and contain them if we're going to win the quarter-final.'

Robinson himself was delighted to have made it to the World Cup after his high-risk strategy of switching codes from league to union two years previously. And he believed England still had plenty in their tank to see off the Welsh. 'The main reason why I moved across to union in the first place was to play in the World Cup,' the Sale Shark explained. 'For all the rugby league test matches I've played for Great Britain, for all the internationals for England's union test team, this is the biggest thing I've ever been involved in. I never realised just how big this was going to be. It's funny, but four years ago, when England were losing the World Cup quarter-final to South Africa in Paris, I didn't even watch the game. I really didn't care about it, you see. But now I feel very different. To come this far and not go all the way doesn't bear thinking about. Wales stand between us and a semi-final. We're well aware that if we under-perform we're on the plane home. The truth is, we haven't hit our best. That's still to come, but it is at this stage that the big performers start to perform. Cometh the

> 'Cometh the hour, cometh the man, as they say. I know this is the biggest game of my life.'
>
> *JASON ROBINSON*

hour, cometh the man, as they say. I know this is the biggest game of my life.'

One player who certainly remembered the 1999 quarter-final was Jonny Wilkinson, about to win his fiftieth cap for England, and, at twenty-four, the youngest player ever to reach that milestone. 'I have been enormously affected by that game,' he admitted. 'It was a huge wake-up call to the pressures of international rugby. Most of all, it brought home to me the fierce nature of the knockout stages of the competition. This is real do-or-die stuff. If we lose on Sunday, it would be at the same stage as four years ago, and that would be even more painful to deal with. It has to be a very realistic prospect. We have played against Wales often enough to know that they are a huge threat. Their performance against the All Blacks surprised a lot of people, but it was no surprise to me.'

Captain Martin Johnson focused on the tenacity the Welsh had displayed against the All Blacks. 'When they went 28–10 down it would have been easy for them to have said it didn't really matter, that they had qualified for the quarter-finals in any case, and they should start conserving themselves for next week. Instead, they gave it a go and got pretty close to pulling off the shock of the World Cup.

'I'll admit I was surprised to see it, but, if I'm honest, I've also been surprised by how Wales have not functioned so well in international rugby in recent years. As a Leicester player, I've never actually won a game in Wales. It's always been really tough. I've never understood why they haven't been able to transfer their club form on to the international stage with the same players. The talent has always been there.

'Judging by the New Zealand game, it's beginning to happen for Wales now. I'm glad they lost, because I wouldn't have wanted to face the All Blacks, at least not in the quarter-final. That said, it's clearly going to be very difficult against this Welsh side, too. It's not just another England–Wales fixture. It's not like the Six Nations, when you know you have another chance within a year at Cardiff or Twickenham. This is the World Cup quarter-final, at a neutral venue, and in the World Cup everything that has gone before tends to be irrelevant. I don't see the game being decided until the final quarter, maybe the last ten minutes. The pressure is all on us. Nobody expects Wales to beat us, so they have nothing to lose. We must make sure we give Wales our full focus. Anything less and they will beat us.'

Johnson admitted that the scheduling of the match at prime time in the evening was a source of some frustration for him and the rest of the England

> 'I don't see the game being decided until the final quarter, maybe the last ten minutes.'
> *MARTIN JOHNSON*

team. 'You just want to get on with it,' he said. 'There's a great deal of hanging around. You try to relax, get some extra sleep, find things to do, but really all you want to do is run out into the stadium and start playing.'

The 1999 Grand Slam defeat by Wales was occupying Clive Woodward's mind on the day before the big match. Despite all the emphatic wins since then, that afternoon at Wembley had remained firmly in his thoughts ever since. 'We weren't too smart that day,' the head coach conceded. 'We didn't deserve to win. It's not the victories I tend to remember, it's the defeats. So there's going to be a huge fear factor about this game. We are at the serious end of this tournament now. It requires a completely different mindset. That's what makes it so exciting. Basically, we can either be flying to Sydney come Monday to prepare for the semi-final, or we'll be flying home to London. We're going to have to make sure it's the Sydney plane we're catching.

'Wales were fantastic [against New Zealand],'he continued. 'They are having a good World Cup and they have nothing to lose on Sunday. I don't happen to agree with the view that they might struggle to get up for another week. In fact, exactly the opposite. They'll be confident coming into this game. You can get a feel for how good a team is by looking at their bench. The Wales bench is looking very strong. Any team who can leave out the likes of Martyn Williams, who always plays well against us, Kevin Morgan and Ceri Sweeney must be good.

'All the past weekend's games have shown that the favourite–underdog tag has been blown away. Out of Australia–Ireland, All Blacks–Wales, Scotland–Fiji, and England–Samoa previously, the underdog could easily have won in all of them. It's not going smoothly for any of the so-called stronger teams.'

Woodward hoped that the Samoan experience, and indeed South Africa before that, had stood England in good stead for the knockout stages. 'From a coaching point of view, it shouldn't be a factor, but the tournament is proving that it is,' he explained. 'If you haven't had some serious games going into the really big one you can sometimes get caught. We know we're not playing at our best, but the confidence of the team will kick in this week, and, anyway, I'd rather be saying this now than sitting around after a game we'd lost. I hope we can do what we've been doing over the last twelve months and move up a gear, which we need to do. We are a bit behind, but we are winning and improving. The bigger the game and the so-called pressure, the better we perform.'

Just a few blocks away in the centre of Brisbane, Wales were making their final preparations. Coach Steve Hansen had been bold in selection, boosted by his players' performances the week before. 'The players didn't die with the music in them,' he explained. 'They sang their hearts out and played as well as they could. We competed really, really well, and in the end just ran out of petrol; not because we're not fit enough, but because we don't play at that intensity often enough. There's been the normal reaction in Wales to a good performance. People have got excited and of course expectations have gone through the roof, but that's a good thing. We've now got to saddle the euphoria and use it to our best advantage. As for England, they're inclined to say nice things about the opposition, probably to put us off the scent. They have come to win the tournament. They're also the most professional team in the tournament. We've got to concentrate on what we've got to do and make sure when we kick off we're up for it.'

On the eve of the game, England suffered a double injury blow. Josh Lewsey was ruled out after pulling his hamstring during Saturday's training session. Obviously, especially considering his performance the previous week, Lewsey was a major loss, but then came the news that the man who was to replace him, Iain Balshaw, had also been forced to withdraw because of a sore knee. For most teams, this would have been devastating, but England's strength in depth came to their rescue. Dan Luger leapfrogged from out of the squad, to on to the bench, to the starting fifteen in a matter of hours. Hardly a bad second reserve to have up your sleeve. To accommodate Luger on the right wing, Jason Robinson would switch to full-back, where he had won most of his England caps.

'It's very disappointing to lose both Lewsey and Balshaw, but neither of them is quite right, and I need players at a hundred per cent for this match,' Woodward explained. 'Dan Luger is an outstanding player in his own right, so we are lucky to have him coming into the team.'

Woodward was absolutely correct in his judgement. England did need to be at 100 per cent against Wales.

Come eight o'clock on Sunday night, the Welsh hit the ground running in the Suncorp Stadium in Brisbane. Leading 10–3 at half-time, they would go on to outscore England by three tries to one, but would lose the match thanks to a second-half revival inspired by an inspired half-time substitution and the near-impeccable goal-kicking of Jonny Wilkinson. The stand-off's five second-half penalties and conversion, added to his first half-effort and a late, late drop goal when the match was won, gave him a personal tally of 23 points. Wilkinson's accumulation of points made the final score look comfortable enough, but the match was still very much in the balance with minutes remaining after Martyn Williams had touched down for Wales' third try.

If Wilkinson eventually emerged as the English hero, he certainly didn't start the match that way. Early on, he struck the post with a relatively simple penalty, and the signs were ominous, because the Welsh were taking the match by the scruff of the neck. Fortunately for England, Stephen Jones then hit the upright with his first kick at goal, and Wilkinson managed to slot his second penalty to give England the lead, somewhat against the run of play. But this only seemed to spur on the Welsh, who were playing with the same abandon they'd shown against New Zealand, spinning the ball out wide at every opportunity.

And England were not exactly making life difficult for them. The first of several strange tactical decisions involved Ben Cohen kicking for the corner to Neil Back. Cohen is usually the recipient of such kicks, and his height and athleticism make him an ideal target man. For all his other attributes, Back doesn't enjoy the same physical advantages. Moreover, in taking the quick tap and then punting cross-field, Cohen had robbed Wilkinson of the chance of a straightforward kick at goal, which would have stretched England's slender lead.

A few minutes later, Wilkinson himself, with options left and right, attempted a drop goal which never came close. They might have been leading, but for all the world it looked like England were panicking. And, in a trice, they had a reason to, because Wales breached the English defence for the first time with what was considered by many to be the try of the tournament.

It began with yet another odd tactical kick from England. Mike Tindall put in a cross-field punt, and one can only assume that he had not spotted it was Ben Kay rather than Dan Luger who was patrolling the wing. Against the big lock stood Shane Williams, one of the quickest, nimblest players in rugby, who had caused the All Blacks no end of problems the week before. Having intercepted the ball, Williams launched the Welsh on a side-stepping, weaving move that included Gareth Thomas and Gareth Cooper before the winger seized the ball again and flipped it inside for the supporting Stephen Jones to score.

Then, four minutes later, Wales punished England again. A kick was hoisted upfield for Shane Williams to chase. A backtracking Cohen got to the ball first but then, with no support, he conceded a penalty. Wales bravely ignored the chance of 3 points by opting to kick for touch in the corner. From the ensuing line-out they formed a powerful ruck which gave their captain, Colin Charvis, the chance to barge his way over the try line. Stephen Jones missed his second conversion of the night, but Wales's well-deserved 7-point lead at half-time still looked daunting, as they were certainly in the ascendancy.

Something had to be done, and quickly, if England were to save the game and salvage their World Cup campaign. At times like this a good coach earns his money, and Woodward made a brave tactical decision during the half-time break. He withdrew an unconvincing Dan Luger, moved centre Mike Tindall out on to the wing, and slotted Mike Catt into the centre. Woodward's hunch was that Catt's incisive running could cause problems for the Welsh, and his no less skilful boot would allow the subdued Wilkinson to play more creatively.

The trick worked, almost to perfection. The first score of the second half was always going to be crucial, and it fell England's way just four minutes after the break. Until this point, Jason Robinson had been pegged back, but his break from just outside the England twenty-two split the Welsh defence wide open. His blistering pace took him all the way to the Welsh twenty-two. With Robinson's side-step, he might well have scored himself, but he wisely off-loaded to a grateful Will Greenwood. The centre still had some work to do, but his strength saw him over the line, in spite of the attentions of Wales's burly full-back, Gareth Thomas. This, Greenwood's thirtieth try for England, saw him draw level with Jerry Guscott. Only Rory Underwood now stood ahead of him now in the English try-scorers' league table (although, admittedly, Underwood wouldn't be sweating yet, as his forty-nine touchdowns was still a long way off). Greenwood had bettered Underwood in one statistic, though: his seventh try against the Welsh wiped the Leicester Tiger's mark from the record books.

Although the try was in the corner, Wilkinson slotted home the conversion with comparative ease. In a seemingly treacherous position at half-time, England had drawn level almost immediately, and from this point until the final ten minutes they would dictate the game. No more tries came their way, but this was mainly because Wales, under increasing pressure, began to concede penalties. Two came within seven minutes, and Wilkinson nudged England into a 6-point lead. A dazed Greenwood left the field shortly afterwards, to be replaced by Stuart Abbott, but it made little difference. By then Catt was making a telling contribution, and Wilkinson, as a result, was flourishing. He found the target again in the 56th minute and on the hour. His sixth penalty followed shortly after and meant that in 22 minutes England had scored 22 unanswered points.

Wales, to their credit, made one last, desperate attempt to get back into the game. A high, teasing cross-field punt from Iestyn Harris saw Shane Williams take on Lawrence Dallagio, unsupported in the corner. Williams, the smallest man on the pitch, leapt to such a height that he managed to knock the ball out of the hands of one of the tallest. Dallaglio then fell to the ground. Martyn Williams, on for Jonathan Thomas, was the quickest to reach the ball and fall on it for the try. With Harris taking over from the wayward Stephen Jones and converting successfully, England's lead was down to 8 points.

The comeback stalled, though. First Harris missed a penalty, then Wales spurned the chance of another and punted for a line-out in the corner instead. No try resulted this time, and the large Welsh contingent started to rue missed opportunities. But England more than held their own in the last few minutes, and Wilkinson's drop goal, the last kick of the match, set the seal on what had been a pulsating quarter-final.

Afterwards, Clive Woodward was happy to have made it through to the last four, but far from content with his team's performance. 'We're not playing well, but we're winning these games through sheer bloody-mindedness,' he declared. 'If we can get a bit more nous in our game and keep the bloody-mindedness we'll beat the French. But if we play like we did tonight, we'll have no chance next weekend. Clearly France are now red-hot favourites. There were some pretty harsh words said at half-time, but I think we got the message.'

> ## 'We're not playing well, but we're winning these games through sheer bloody-mindedness.'
>
> *CLIVE WOODWARD*

Martin Johnson was equally disappointed in the way his team had performed. 'We battled back and took control in the second half, but it was too sloppy to be satisfied,' said the lock forward. 'Our line-out was poor again and we were hurried off the ball. Their defence was on top of us in the first half. I was disappointed that we panicked like that. Full credit to Wales.'

Wales, though, were not satisfied themselves, even though everyone was telling them they'd exceeded expectations for the second week in a row. 'The game was there to be won the whole way,' insisted their coach, Steve Hansen. 'It was a real contest and if England are honest with themselves it could have gone either way. We really wanted to ask questions of them, of their fitness and their ability to move the ball around the park.'

Jonny Wilkinson was straightforward in his assessment. 'We didn't start well and, because of that, we had to do a lot of defending,' he admitted. 'In the second half we were far better and we managed to come through. That tells you a great deal about the character of the side.'

That second-half performance, though, was made possible by the introduction of Mike Catt. One of the game's great survivors, Catt was happy just to be at the World Cup after his year of injuries and near tragedy at home. He had predicted that if he got his chance he would take it, and he had been true to his word.

> ## 'I hope I have done enough now to get a crack in the semi-final.'
>
> *MIKE CATT*

'I really enjoyed being out there,' he explained afterwards. 'The only instructions I received were to go out there and play my usual game. It was that straightforward, and that is what I did. I hope I have done enough now to get a crack in the semi-final.'

That match would be against France the following Sunday, this time in Sydney, in the magnificent 80,000-seater Telstra Stadium that housed the 2000 Olympics. Clive Woodward's assessment was correct: France had demolished Ireland in a one-sided quarter-final and remained, perhaps even more so than New Zealand, the form team of the World Cup. They would be the favourites to reach the final, and England would have to find a few extra gears to overcome them.

At least England had reached the semi-finals, though, which was already one round better than four years previously. 'We're where we wanted to be,' concluded Woodward. 'We haven't been at our best, but we haven't lost a game yet in this World Cup, either. I believe we'll beat France.'

The World Cup had suddenly found extra heat.

Chapter 10

ENGLAND 24–7 FRANCE

Sunday 16 November
at the Telstra Stadium, Sydney

England: Lewsey, Robinson, Greenwood, Catt (Tindall, 71), Cohen, Wilkinson, Dawson (Bracken, 40–1, 72), Woodman (Leonard, 80), Thompson (West, 80), Vickery (Leonard, 4–6), Johnson (Captain), Kay, Hill (Moody, 75), Back, Dallaglio

Pens: Wilkinson 5
Drop Goals: Wilkinson 3

France: Brusque, Rougerie, Marsh, Jauzion, Dominici (sin-bin, 27–37; Poîtrenaud, 37), Michalak (Merceron, 65), Galthié (Captain), Crenca (Milloud, 63), Ibañez, Marconnet, Pelous, Thion, Betsen (sin-bin, 54–64; Labit, 64), Magne, Harinordoquy

Try: Betsen
Con: Michalak

Referee: P. O'Brien (New Zealand)

Attendance: 82,346

MATCH STATISTICS
Possession: England 60%, France 40%
Territory: England 60%, France 40%
Tackles Made (Attempted): England 52 (61), France 121 (138)
Line-outs Won: England 16 from 19, France 18 from 22
Rucks and Mauls: England 94, France 34

With the World Cup reaching boiling point, it was hardly surprising that England were now not going to have things all their own way. The good news, of course, was that they had qualified for the semi-final. The bad news, or at least it appeared that way immediately after the quarter-finals, was that the team they would meet in that semi-final was France, who had illuminated the tournament with their flair and attacking rugby. Head coach Clive Woodward knew his team had to improve considerably to quell the French, and he also realised that the best way to do this was to field his strongest possible starting fifteen, something he had been unable to do since the first pool game against Georgia.

With doubts remaining over the injured Josh Lewsey and Iain Balshaw, Woodward wanted to leave nothing to chance. Late on the Sunday night he called the Leicester utility back Austin Healey and asked him to make his way over to Australia. 'Austin is being flown over as a precaution,' Woodward explained. 'We will continue to monitor the fitness of Josh and Iain over the next twenty-four hours.'

Healey's last visit to Australia had been on the 2001 Lions tour, where his outspoken attacks on the Wallabies, the country and, in particular, lock Justin Harrison made him a marked man Down Under. 'I wonder what reception I'll get this time,' Healey mused, shortly before boarding his plane. 'I know that I might be flying back again later in the week, but at least this time I'm fit, should they need me.'

A day later, things started to look up for England. Richard Hill, out of the World Cup since the first pool game against Georgia with a hamstring twinge that had refused to clear up, finally declared himself fit and available for selection. It was just the tonic England needed. For all the sterling efforts of Lewis Moody and, to a lesser extent, Joe Worsley, Hill had been sorely missed. 'I've had my moments when I feared the worst,' a relieved Hill admitted. 'There have also been times when I've wondered whether I was going to run out of time, but it's great to be able to say I'm fit now.'

Meanwhile, Woodward was facing the media flak concerning England's World Cup performances, notably against Samoa and Wales. 'It's not a case of anxiety, but it is a bit perplexing,' he said. 'We've got to accept the criticism because it is due. We are playing on too narrow a front, which is unlike England, and we have lost a bit of concentration, which, again, is not like us. But this tournament is all about winning, and we've won all our games so far.'

Mike Catt filled most column inches in the days after the quarter-final. Would he be selected to start the semi-final after his stunning contribution in the second half against Wales? The consensus was that he had swung the game England's way, while, incredibly, Jonny Wilkinson had seemed to let the weight of expectation get the better of him.

Catt's transformation from being initially outside Woodward's World Cup plans to becoming a likely starter against France had been remarkable. The centre himself put it down to a total lack of expectation on his part. 'I've got no pressure on me at the moment,' he explained. 'I haven't had the pressures of the past six months on my back. I'm capable of doing whatever is asked of me. I'm thoroughly enjoying it. Whatever comes my way comes my way. It's good fun at the moment.'

If Catt was riding on the crest of a wave, though, Wilkinson seemed to need some support, and he received it from the England management. 'Wilkinson had an outstanding game [against Wales],' Woodward stated. 'You have to see Jonny as a completely different number ten from anyone else in the world. Because he is so aggressive he wants to get involved all the time. Jonny hasn't changed since I've known him and I don't want him to. He's the world's best number ten. He will be playing against the French and he will have a major influence on the game.'

Wilkinson's half-back partner, Matt Dawson, was also quick to defend a young man who was experiencing almost the first harsh criticism in a glittering career. 'Being labelled the best player in the world means that you get more attention than anyone else,' said the scrum-half. 'By his own admission, he has not played as well as he can, but that is symptomatic of the team. Jonny plays as he sees it. For me, as scrum-half, Mike Catt brings that second option as a number ten. If Jonny is doing things like clearing rucks, having another fly-half makes a huge difference.' As for England, 'I don't think the style of play has deteriorated,' said Dawson, 'but we've probably just plateaued a bit. We've not improved as we've wanted to, but I think the twenty-five minutes we played at the start of the second half [in the quarter-final] was the best we've played at this World Cup.'

The man in question seemed to be taking it all in his stride. 'I've not got a huge opinion of my own game at the moment, other than to say I'm slightly unhappy,' Wilkinson explained. 'I wouldn't say I have a corner to turn, and I wouldn't say I'm playing well. I'm digging in and looking to improve. The only pressure I feel is that it's my duty to make the most of the time I've got. I'm proud of the way we've fought and won the games. It's not quite right yet, but we're working on it.'

But there were even more serious issues

'I'm digging in and looking to improve ... I'm proud of the way we've fought and won the games. It's not quite right yet, but we're working on it.'

JONNY WILKINSON

than the form of their stand-off concerning England in the run-up to the semi-final. Prop Phil Vickery underlined the team's focus when asked how he viewed the prospect of playing in a World Cup final. 'It hasn't even entered my head,' he answered. 'If we start thinking beyond Sunday, we will be in more trouble and we are in enough trouble as it is. The French scrum is undeniably the best in the world. Whenever you play the French as a front-row forward the fear hits you. We certainly aren't going to run away from it and, while we haven't played particularly well as a team, nobody within the camp is pressing the panic button. When things are not going well everyone looks for excuses. Don't get me wrong, we are not playing well, but nobody needs any motivating for this weekend's match. You'd give everything you've got to win. You'd give your life, if need be. I just hope I'm among those given the opportunity.'

> 'You'd give everything you've got to win. You'd give your life, if need be.'
>
> *PHIL VICKERY*

Phil Vickery would have to wait longer than expected to see if that opportunity was coming his way, because Woodward delayed the team announcement until he was sure of Lewsey's and Balshaw's fitness. Austin Healey, who had just arrived at the team's Manly hotel base in the north of Sydney, was therefore asked to stay a while, although, under World Cup regulations, he was not allowed to join up with the England squad unless someone was formally withdrawn.

Martin Johnson, meanwhile, countered growing claims from former Australian internationals in the local media that his team was showing its age. 'Brisbane had the hottest conditions we have seen in the tournament and it had an effect on us,' he conceded. 'But we came through strongly and won the game. It's cooler here in Sydney, though, and we're training in the evenings, which is a great help. Age is not a problem. The Australians suggested this before we played them in June and after the game they said how good we were. If you are playing badly, then people will question your age. If you don't play an all-singing, all-dancing game, people think it's not great, but it's about winning the games. I'm almost boring myself making this point. It's only ever about winning.

> 'I'm almost boring myself making this point. It's only ever about winning.'
>
> *MARTIN JOHNSON*

'It's much better to be talking about a disappointing victory than to be sat at home talking about being beaten. We won a World Cup quarter-final and people are saying: "Oh dear, you're not playing very well." I'll tell you this – Wales would love to have won that game and be able to say that. As for France, they have a lot of class and a lot of speed in there. They are the form team of the World Cup. It's a tough challenge. We could play well and still lose. We're not going to be able to play poorly and pull off a win. France are too good for that. But it's not a game now we're expected to win. So winning by a point will do.'

By the Thursday, Clive Woodward was in the happy position of naming what he considered to be his first-choice starting fifteen (and, indeed, a first-choice bench). The only surprise, or at least it would have been before the quarter-final win over Wales, was the selection of Mike Catt at inside centre. The unlucky Mike Tindall was dropped to the bench. With the dynamic French to face, the main cause of concern over this decision was in respect to England's defence. However, defensive coach Phil Larder insisted, 'Mike Catt isn't as physical a defender as Tindall, but he is pretty astute and intelligent. The defence will not be weakened.'

Woodward also had no doubt that he'd made the right selection. 'Catty has come along very well in the past couple of games,' he said. 'We also want to get some width in our game, which we have always been doing until this World Cup. I see no gamble at all. You saw he played outstandingly in the second half against Wales. It is the correct balance for us to beat France, which I believe we will do.'

Catt himself was relishing the chance to make a difference. 'The side has done exceptionally well in the past two years, but maybe there's a bit of staleness in there,' he argued. 'I hope to bring some freshness and a bit of perspective into the game. Maybe I can take a little pressure off so that Jonny can roam the field a little bit more, and I can take a little bit of the heat off him when it comes to a kicking game as well. I'll fit in quite nicely.'

Catt was one of a handful of England players surviving from the 1995 World Cup semi-final, when a Jonah Lomu-inspired New Zealand trounced Will Carling's side. In particular, he is remembered for being trampled over by Lomu for the All Blacks' first try. 'I look at that particular game and you had the likes of Tim Rodber and Martin Johnson trying to tackle Jonah and they were eighteen stones and I was only thirteen stones, so I probably didn't have a chance anyway,' he admitted. His explanation for his remarkably relaxed manner was simple: 'Sport is a fickle business and, while rugby had been everything to me until my family came along, the more recent worries have made me change my outlook completely. I still give it my best, but I don't worry about it the way I used to. There are more important things in life than rugby.'

Mike Tindall seemed to adhere to Catt's philosophy himself, as he took his demotion on the chin. 'You haven't got time to be feeling sorry for yourself,' he said. 'It's tough and it hurts but there's nothing I can do about it. You can't afford to be disappointed, otherwise you won't be able to do yourself justice when the time comes. Besides, there's some reasoning behind it in that Mike bossed the game when he came on. He helped Jonny and kicked superbly. If people are targeting Jonny and pressurising his kicks, it gives us an option.'

In total, the starting fifteen showed four changes from that which had narrowly defeated the Welsh, with Trevor Woodman trading places with Jason Leonard at loose head, and Richard Hill and Josh Lewsey returning from injury. On the bench, Martin Corry would be coming in for Simon Shaw. If Leonard came on to the field at some point during the semi-final, he would earn a world-record-breaking 112th cap.

With Balshaw and Lewsey fit to play, Austin Healey duly returned to England. He had played for the Leicester Tigers on Saturday, took the Australia-bound flight on Sunday, arrived on Tuesday afternoon and was on his way back to England by Wednesday teatime, in readiness for his club's Powergen Cup game the following Saturday.

A happy Hill, back in the starting fifteen for the first time in over a month, talked of his frustration of the previous few weeks. 'The hardest bit was not putting on the shirt,' he said. 'There was no ultimatum from the management, but I did have my down patches. There are only so many times you can be given a lifeline. It was towards the end of last week that I began to feel comfortable again, so much so that I packed my boots and gumshield for last Sunday's game just in case.'

As for England's supposedly stuttering campaign so far, Hill was unconcerned. 'Fundamentally, I don't think we have gone massively wrong,' he added. 'If we had, we wouldn't still be in the tournament. It is just a case of sharpening up certain aspects of our play, applying more pressure on the opposition and playing the game that we want to play.'

'All three of us in the front row really treasure the scrum as a good attacking weapon ... The way we look at every scrum is like it's a special occasion.'

STEVE THOMPSON

Hooker Steve Thompson was relishing the chance to have another crack at the French. In the four tests he had played against France he had enjoyed two wins and suffered two defeats. They were the only team he had ever lost to in his international career. 'It's always a very hard match when we play them and always very close,' the twenty-five-year-old insisted. 'It's always a hard scrummaging confrontation against them. They're very much a similar team to South Africa. All three of us in the front row really treasure the scrum

Kick-off in the quarter-final, v Wales at the Suncorp Stadium, 9th November 2003 (*Cameron Spencer/Getty Images*).

The introduction of Mike Catt into the centre at half-time worked almost to perfection. His inspired running caused a headache for the Welsh; he also allowed Jonny Wilkinson to play more creatively (*Nick Laham/Getty Images*).

The forwards, above, clash in the scrum (*Darren England/Getty Images*); below, Will Greenwood scores England's only try of the game (*Adam Pretty/Getty Images*); right, Jason Robinson darts the length of the pitch to create the try (*David Rogers/Getty Images*).

Anti-clockwise from main photo: Martin Johnson addresses the England huddle before the match of their lives, the semi-final against France (*Daniel Berehulak/Getty Images*); Matt Dawson in inspired form against the French (*Chris McGrath/Gettty Images*); Jason Leonard runs on to the pitch for a world-record 112th cap (*Jon Buckle/Getty Images*).

Jonny Wilkinson's drop goals, penalties and conversions accounted for all of England's 24 points against the French (above: the first points on the board for England) (*Mark Nolan/Daniel Berehulak/ Getty Images*); right, Captain Martin Johnson struggles with Christophe Dominici of France (*Daniel Berehulak/Getty Images*).

England		France
0	Tries	1
0	Conversions	1
4	Penalties	0
3	Drop Goals	0
21	Score	7

Second Half

The world's greatest no.10 with the last kick of the match (*David Rogers/Getty Images*); Clive Woodward and Andy Robinson are calm in the week before the final (*David Rogers/Getty Images*).

as a good attacking weapon that can wear down the opposition. The way we look at every scrum is like it's a special occasion.'

Jason Leonard, on the bench but still looking forward immensely to the forthcoming challenge, further explained the importance of the battle. 'It starts with the very first scrum of the game, and it continues until the very last,' he said. 'We're not talking feet here. We're talking inches. It's imperative we don't give an inch, we don't give France any kind of advantage at all. The front row hasn't changed that much, in truth. Our role is to provide set-piece play for our team-mates, and to disrupt the opposition's set pieces. It's nice to get your hands on the ball and have a little run, but if we don't get the first bit right, we won't get the chance to run.'

Will Greenwood was another keen admirer on the French. 'When I'm not actually playing against them, there's nothing I like more than watching France,' he said. 'They are clearly a world-class side. I don't have many rugby videos, but I do have the 1999 semi-final between New Zealand and France, and it was superb to see how the French ran the All Blacks ragged. We love the games against France. We love to hate them and they love to hate us. It's a kind of hate–hate relationship.'

> **'We love to hate them and they love to hate us. It's a kind of hate–hate relationship.'**
>
> *WILL GREENWOOD*

Greenwood was unfazed by the challenge of forging an effective partnership with a new team-mate in the centre. 'It's obvious that what Catty brought to the field in the second half against Wales was a superb kicking game, and at ten and twelve that gives us great options. Sometimes it's better for me to slot in at twelve and Catty to thirteen, and that's how we'll play. It's not as if we're going on the hoof, but at certain times you need to adapt and change. France have two guys at nine and ten who can control the game as well as anyone in the world. In the defensive meeting we said that they can play wide, narrow and up the middle, so that doesn't leave a lot of places they don't attack! We're not going to try to read too much into how they're going to play, as we're never quite sure which French team will turn up. They can be absolutely brilliant in all areas of the field and we just have to focus.'

Neil Back knew only too well how good the French could be, but he preferred to concentrate on England, a team he clearly believed would reach the final. 'We have a confidence borne out of what we've achieved,' he announced. 'We've won nineteen out of our last twenty games, the one defeat by one point to a full-strength French side, in France, against our second string. If that doesn't give you confidence, I don't know what will.' He was also delighted that the holy trinity of himself, Lawrence Dallaglio and Richard Hill was back in place. 'This is a tried and tested combination,' he argued. 'In fact, we hold the world record for the number of times we have played together as a unit. This tells in World Cup semi-finals. As a combination, we complement one another. Lawrence makes the most runs, I make the most tackles and Hilly is a happy medium between Lawrence and myself. So France know, and we know, that we will be putting them under enormous pressure.'

South of Manly, the French were based on Bondi Beach, a perfect location for those players who seemed intent on topping up their tans when not preparing to meet England. They, too, seemed confident of claiming the win. Flanker Imanol Harinordoquy was fired up. 'Clive Woodward said the French would not pose any problems,' he said. 'That is the kind of declaration that gets me going, because they really believe it.' Stand-off Frérdéric Michalak added: 'Our back row will make life hell for Jonny Wilkinson.' But the French also clearly respected their opposition. 'It will be a huge match,' said lock forward Jerome Thion. Serge Betsen, meanwhile, conceded that Wilkinson was 'the best player in the world and very, very important to England'. And Wilkinson's opposite number Michalak admitted that the English player's example was the one he mostly followed: 'He's the one fly-half with all the attributes. For us youngsters [Michalak was only twenty-one at the time], he's someone good to look up to. He's got all the qualities to be the best player in the world.'

Coach Bernard Laporte had kept the same starting fifteen that had decimated Ireland the previous week in the quarter-final, but made four changes to the bench. Christian Labit came in for Patrick Tabacco and Damien Traille for Brian Liebenberg, while David Auradou replaced the injured Olivier Brouzet, and Clement Poîtrenaud was in for full-back Pepita Elhorga, who returned home to attend his father's funeral. Laporte had gained a reputation for his intelligent coaching, as well as the success he had brought to France. He was not going to fall into any traps now. 'England are favourites,' he insisted. 'Everyone's talking about England being a laborious side, but no one has actually beaten them yet. They play a highly pressurised game and then tend to spread it out wide once they've worn down the opposition. They play a territorial game with clever kicking. They are also strong in line-outs, scrums and their kicking game. The Welsh coach, Steve Hansen, said last week that England's defence had been predictable. Well, all I can say is that he knew a lot about England's defence and has now gone home. I'd like to know a lot less and be in next week's final.'

On the Saturday, Clive Woodward spoke publicly with more emotion than perhaps ever before. All week he had been insisting his team would prevail, and now, just twenty-four hours before the big kick-off, he wanted to ram home his point. 'I strongly believe England will beat France,' he stated. 'We have an outstanding set of players, outstanding leadership, we're fresh, we're very experienced and we know how to win games. Just a look at our track record will confirm this. I have absolutely no doubt that England will step up to the plate. We came here to win the World Cup and we will not be leaving the field until we've made it to the final. Of that we are absolutely determined.'

He was far from finished, either. In Martin Johnson, who would be breaking a World Cup record by playing in his seventeenth successive game, he felt England possessed the best captain in the world. 'He's an outstanding sportsman, a brilliant guy and every member of the team looks up to him,' Woodward explained. 'He's been at the forefront of all England's success in recent years and the whole of English rugby owes him a great debt. I cannot think of another player more deserving to be playing in a World Cup final and that's what we're going to achieve.'

England would be boosted, too, by hundreds of good-luck messages, faxes and emails. Among those sending encouragement was English football's 1966 World Cup-winner, Jack Charlton. 'We got a lovely fax from him,' Woodward revealed. 'He made it very clear it was all about winning, which is our kind of language. I read what he says, and I listen to Martin Johnson, and it doesn't matter how you get there, you just have to get there. We're very conscious of the excitement back at home and also out here in Sydney. The number of white shirts here is a huge motivating force and we're desperate not to let down our thousands of fans in Australia and at home.'

The head coach was unequivocal about what he expected from his players. 'It's time for everyone to front up,' he said. 'We're going to have to play right on the very edge. This is what we've been building up to for a long time. The team is fully aware of the enormity of the game. They want to win it more than any other game they've ever played in their whole lives.'

Unlike the previous week, when England had appeared heavy-legged and tired against Wales after training in the Brisbane heat, Woodward was confident that this time they had got it just right. 'We've tapered down this week and, as a result, are very fresh. The boys are ready. They've been ready all week. They're so experienced now, they know exactly what to do.'

If the team needed any extra motivation, though, Woodward only needed to mention the spectre of the dreaded third-place play-off. 'Believe me,' he said. 'Nobody wants to play in that game. We certainly didn't come here to end up featuring in the play-off. I don't care how we play against France as long as we win. If we play badly and win by a point, then I'm happy. If we play really well and lose, then it will be a very sad night for us.'

Woodward was talking immediately before the first semi-final between Australia and New Zealand, and, going against the common consensus, he named the home team as his favourites for that match. Like England, the Wallabies had been criticised for not producing their best form, but they suddenly found a few extra gears against the All Blacks. In front of a passionate, partisan crowd at the Telstra Stadium, they displayed an impregnable defence, top-notch place-kicking from Elton Flatley and piercing running that stretched New Zealand throughout. By the end, it had become a surprisingly one-sided spectacle.

Come Sunday night, and the balmy weather enjoyed by the two Southern Hemisphere teams the day before had given way to swirling winds, incessant rain and a considerable drop in temperature. Nevertheless, the English fans came in their hordes. Nobody could put a precise number on how many packed inside the Telstra Stadium, but they seemed to outnumber their French counterparts by at least four to one, almost turning this crunch encounter at what was supposed to be a neutral venue into a home game. The support, as Clive Woodward pointed out after the match, certainly played its part in what turned out to be a stunning night for English rugby.

Despite the form that France had displayed coming into this semi-final, England ran out deserved winners thanks to the lethal boot (or rather boots, as his supposedly weaker right was just as crucial as his left on this night) of the 'off-form' Jonny Wilkinson. The much-criticised stand-off answered his critics with five penalty kicks out of eight in extremely difficult kicking conditions, but what truly demoralised France was his new-found appetite for drop goals. French heads had begun to drop long before the final whistle courtesy of the one left-footed and two right-footed kicks that had sailed over the bar.

Yet Wilkinson was the first to acknowledge that the chances he put away were all created by an inspired performance from the English pack. To a man, they held firm against their formidable opponents, but also punched holes through the French defence and forced a catalogue of errors along the way. The front row of Trevor Woodman, Steve Thompson and Phil Vickery hardly yielded an inch all night, while locks Johnson and Ben Kay, and the back row of Back, Dallaglio and Hill (lasting well over an hour in his comeback game), repeatedly made breaks that pegged back France. The backs did their job, too, constructing a defiant wall of defence that simply refused access, with Catt kicking for position and territory alongside Wilkinson.

It wasn't particularly pretty to watch – the terrible playing conditions removed any chance of a spectacle – but semi-finals, as Woodward and Johnson had been saying all week, are simply about winning. Recognised as the worst hurdle at which to fall, England, just like Australia the night before, had got the job done. They had both proved, in the process, that a team who wants to win the World must finish, rather than start, the strongest.

Within a mere four minutes Jason Leonard was trundling on to the pitch to replace a bloodied Vickery. The venerable prop would stay on the field for only two minutes on this occasion, but in doing so he earned his 112th, world-record-breaking cap. He was given another run-out right at the death, and revelled in one of the biggest cheers of the night.

In the 9th minute, Jonny Wilkinson and England were on their way. In wet conditions, with the ball slipping through both sides' hands in almost every phase of play, it was obvious that chances to score points had to be taken at every opportunity. So, rather than trying to spin the play out to the wings, Wilkinson slotted his first drop goal of the night. The ball flew as sweetly off his right boot as it would have done off his left.

However, England were soon given a severe jolt. Within a couple of minutes, France scored what would prove to be the only try of the game through Serge Betsen. Thompson failed to find any of his own men at a line-out on England's twenty-two. Instead, the ball fell into the grateful hands of the Cameroon-born flanker, who made a dash for the line. Jason Robinson looked to have done enough to prevent the score, but, after lengthy deliberation by Australian video referee Andrew Cole, the match referee, Paddy O'Brien, awarded the try. Michalak kicked the conversion, and the French appeared to be living up to their favourite's billing.

'It was my mistake that cost us the try,' Richard Hill was quick and honest enough to admit later. 'It was a missed tackle and it cost us. I didn't let it get me down, though, and I was happy with my performance after that.'

For a while, France continued to have the upper hand. Under pressure, England were infringing, and Les Bleus were given the chance to put real distance between the teams. Twice Michalak had penalty kicks well within his range, and twice the young star of French rugby directed his kick wide. A 3–13 French lead might have rocked England so far back that they'd never recover, but, after the misses, the pendulum began to swing England's way as their forwards took a hold of the game. In the 24th minute, Christophe Dominici, France's flying winger who had been so influential in the French semi-final win over New Zealand four years previously, was yellow-carded after a blatant trip on Jason Robinson. In the process, Dominici injured himself, and when his ten minutes in the sin-bin were up, he was replaced by Clement Poîtrenaud. Wilkinson missed the kick that resulted from the trip, but made amends four minutes later when his high bomb led to Jauzion being caught offside. This time Wilkinson made no mistake with his penalty, and suddenly England were only a point adrift.

France were not quite finished yet, though. Tony Marsh put a grubber kick into the corner for Aurlien Rougerie to chase, and Ben Cohen only just beat the French winger to the ball. It proved to be something of a turning point, because, from then on, England's ascendancy was never seriously challenged. Following a Neil Back break and concerted English pressure, Wilkinson found the target two minutes before the break with a second right-footed drop goal. Soon after, and still before half-time, Wilkinson kicked a brilliant penalty from forty-two metres out. England had not looked like crossing the French line, but they were five points up. As this had been achieved into the teeth of torrential rain and a gale, the omens looked good for England to finish the job with the wind at their backs in the second half.

The win may have been on the cards from this point, but the manner in which it was achieved devastated France. Wilkinson missed two early second-half penalty chances in the testing conditions, but in the 53rd minute Betsen handed England a golden opportunity. The heroic try-scorer became the villain when he pole-axed Wilkinson some considerable time after the ball had left the stand-off's boot. 'That's absolutely crazy. He got the kick away,' said an incredulous O'Brien as he brandished the yellow card and sent Betsen to the sidelines for ten minutes. Combined with Dominici's earlier sin-binning, France therefore had to play a quarter of the match with only fourteen men.

To add insult to injury, Wilkinson picked himself up and found the target from the resulting penalty. Then, five minutes later, after a Back break, he struck his third drop goal, this time with the regulation left boot. England were eleven points up and France hadn't scored for almost an hour. The French were buckling under considerable pressure, just as the All Blacks had in the other semi-final the day before. Their play had become error-strewn, and the English defence was successfully nullifying arguably the most potent attacking force in the World Cup. And even when they did manufacture even the glimmer of an opening, suddenly, for the first time in the tournament, the French could not rely on Michalak to convert it into points. Soon after he missed his fourth successive kick at goal, he was replaced by the more experienced Merceron. Michalak had shone in this World Cup, and undoubtedly would do so again, but on a rainy night in Sydney his spark had been extinguished, at least for a time.

By then, Wilkinson had already added his fourth penalty of the evening after the old enemy of French success – their own indiscipline – had reared its head again. Time was fast running out for France, and their mood would hardly have been improved by seeing the eager Mike Tindall sprinting on to the field in place of Mike Catt in the 71st minute, and Lewis Moody, who had played such a big part in the tournament, coming on for the understandably fatigued Richard Hill. Willing and accomplished replacement though Moody was, Hill, yet again, had underlined his importance to the England team.

Hill, yet again, had underlined his importance to the England team.

With eight minutes remaining, Wilkinson kicked his fifth penalty when

France were penalised for not releasing the ball. The stand-off had now scored every one of England's twenty-four points. And that's the way it would finish, with one of the most prolific teams in world rugby shut out for over seventy minutes, and an 'out-of-form' stand-off putting in a display that anyone else would have been hard-pressed to match. All that was missing from England was a try for the fans in the stadium to cheer, and they almost managed it. Tindall got his hands on Wilkinson's clever chip over the flat French defence, but the centre was adjudged to have been held up over the line. Of course, it made little difference, as the game was already long won. However, when Paddy O'Brien blew the final whistle, England avoided the lap of honour that had been taken the day before by the victorious Wallabies, and headed for the tunnel. The game may have been won, but the tournament had not been . . . yet.

Clive Woodward was obviously delighted, but also keen to keep his and his squad's feet on the ground. 'I'm very proud of everyone involved tonight: my staff, especially the players, and also the eight not involved in the twenty-two-man squad,' he said. 'Their support behind the scenes has been fantastic and now we can look forward to a World Cup final.

'Ever since we beat South Africa, if I'm honest, the French have been in our minds. It was important to have got to the semi-final stage, but, as I kept on saying all last week, this was another level, a one-off game, and one we prepared for to win. The conditions didn't make it very pleasant, but I don't see it as anything in our favour. You have to be able to play in all conditions, and I believe we would have beaten France if it had been bone dry and warm out there tonight.'

On the prospect of facing Australia, the team he had astutely predicted would make the final, Woodward said, 'I'm actually delighted to be facing Australia, because they are a quality team; they are the host nation; they've put on a wonderful World Cup tournament; and it's a great North–South battle between two great and old adversaries. We've won the last four games against them and we now hope to make it five in a row.'

Finally, the head coach insisted on making a special point about his record-breaking prop. 'Jason received the biggest round of applause in the dressing room immediately afterwards,' Woodward revealed. 'I'm so glad that the PA announcer notified the crowd when he came on about what it all meant. A huge moment of sporting history was made out there tonight.'

Assistant coach Andy Robinson echoed his boss's sentiments: 'What can I say? It was a magnificent performance. Once again there were questions being raised about whether this team, and especially the pack, were too old, and once again they went out and performed. I have total respect for all the guys.'

Martin Johnson reflected, 'You've got one chance to be in a World Cup final, and one chance for the ultimate prize, so we knew what we had to do. We saw how Australia got ahead in the first semi-final, and we knew it would be hard to be trying to catch up. It was nice to get the first points on the board, and even though Betsen's try was obviously a setback, I was pleased with the way we reacted. The guys basically said, "Forget about it, and let's move on." I was confident that we'd stop them scoring after that. Once we gained a bit of a lead it was always going to be difficult for France to come back in those conditions. That's when they started to grow frustrated, which is why mistakes crept in. We would have taken a one-point victory tonight, no problem. There was a lot of expectation all week, and we asked the guys to play the biggest game of their lives. That's exactly what they did, but next week they'll have to produce an even bigger performance to beat the Wallabies.'

The French, for their part, were dejected but magnanimous in defeat. 'The better team won tonight,' admitted their outgoing captain, scrum-half Fabien Galthié. 'We were in the game for the first twenty minutes but after that we made too many mistakes and we were under too much pressure.' His coach, Bernard Laporte, having thanked Galthié for his contribution to French rugby, also conceded that his team were second best on the night. 'The weather conditions didn't help us, for sure, but we must be able to adapt to all conditions,' he said. 'It was us who made the errors, but when you are under the sort of pressure England placed us under, errors happen. Jonny Wilkinson had a great match. I wish he was French.'

> **'Jonny Wilkinson had a great match. I wish he was French.'**
>
> *BERNARD LAPORTE*

Luckily for England, he's not.

Six years earlier Clive Woodward had taken the reins of the England team. Since then they had one failed World Cup campaign, two Six Nations titles and a Grand Slam under their belts. In this World Cup they'd won six games in a row, and now they were six days away from the final. They would be playing in the biggest game in the history of British rugby, and could play a part in the greatest achievement in British sport since the 1966 Football World Cup Final. The week ahead was not going to be short on drama.

Chapter 11

WORLD CUP FINAL, ENGLAND 20–17 AUSTRALIA

(after extra time)

Saturday 22 November at the Telstra Stadium, Sydney

England: Lewsey (Balshaw, 85), Robinson, Greenwood, Tindall (Catt, 78), Cohen, Wilkinson, Dawson, Woodman, Thompson, Vickery (Leonard, 80), Johnson (Captain), Kay, Hill (Moody, 93), Back, Dallaglio

Try: Robinson
Pens: Wilkinson 4
Drop Goal: Wilkinson

Australia: Rogers, Sailor (Roff, 70), Mortlock, Flatley, Tuqiri, Larkham (Giteau, 20–30, 55–63, 85–93), Gregan (Captain), Young (Dunning, 92), Cannon (Paul, 56), Baxter, Harrison, Sharpe (Giffin, 47), Smith, Waugh, Lyons (Cockbain, 56)

Try: Tuqiri
Pens: Flatley 4

Referee: A. Watson (South Africa)

Attendance: 82,957

MATCH STATISTICS
Possession: England 58%, Australia 42%
Territory: England 54%, Australia 46%
Tackles Made (Attempted): England 139 (158), Australia 161 (185)
Line-outs Won (Lost): England 28 (9), Australia 23 (5)
Rucks and Mauls: England 101, Australia 74

They were calling it the 'Dream Final' as soon as the two opponents were known. Australia, two-time World Cup-winners, were trying to become the first country successfully to defend the crown. In their way would be the world's best team (according to the latest rankings), England, the old enemy and Australia's greatest rivals. It was the final most neutrals had wanted to see: a showdown between South and North; the team of the nineties against potentially the team of the new millennium; George Gregan against Martin Johnson; Eddie Jones against Clive Woodward. And, as if any extra spice were needed, it gave England the chance to avenge their defeat by the Australians on home soil in the 1991 World Cup Final.

Woodward, one of the few who had predicted that the Wallabies would reach the final, was pleased that the World Cup's last match would be played out by the two old foes. 'I'm delighted we're playing Australia for two reasons,' he explained. 'They've done a brilliant job in organising this event and they have a squad of real quality. I've said all along that they would be the team to beat and now we're the only team left with a chance of doing it. When the tournament began, I would have said this was my dream final. We have one objective and we're now one game away from achieving it. We certainly haven't come out here to finish second.' Although England have won all four tests against the Wallabies since defeat in Sydney in 1999, Woodward was still cautious. 'This will be a complete one-off,' he said. 'I hope we can make it five, but I don't think those previous matches will have any bearing on Saturday.'

And so began the most memorable, and sometimes frenetic, week in English rugby history. Back home, the country started to appreciate that one of their elite sporting teams had reached a World Cup final. That was a major achievement in itself, of course, for a nation that had had only three World Cup Cricket finals (all lost) and that 1991 Twickenham defeat to shout about since 1966 at Wembley, when the football team had actually managed to win something. With talk building of Woodward emulating Sir Alf Ramsay and Martin Johnson taking on the mantle of the late, great Bobby Moore, the head coach was happy to talk of his own memories of that summer day back in sixties. 'I watched it with my dad at the RAF station in Yorkshire where he was based,' he recalled. 'I have never forgotten the team that won it. I was big into football in those days: I didn't start playing rugby until I was fifteen.

'Having lived in Australia for five years, I can say that England is probably even more sports crazy than Australia. My only goal when I left my business to take this job six years ago was to make England the best team in the world and win this thing. Now we have a real chance of doing exactly that. Since we lost in Paris two seasons ago, we have won twenty-one out of twenty-two matches, the exception being the single-point defeat by our second team in Marseille in the summer. We have a very experienced team who know how to win test matches, and this week we have to take everything in our stride. In six years we have been through some fantastic times and had some bitter experiences through defeats, but there came a stage a couple of years ago when all the learning had been done. A lot of this is down to Martin Johnson, the best captain in world rugby by a long way. But he would be the first to acknowledge that he has brilliant support. There are a lot of brains out there, with people like Dallaglio, Back, Hill, Dawson and Wilkinson. I have never seen them panic at any time during the last few years, not even when we went fourteen points down to Australia at Twickenham last season. That was the best example of how not to panic and claw your way back into the match.

> '**The players have got one shot at this, but they are the most talented group of players English rugby has ever had.**'
>
> *CLIVE WOODWARD*

'The players have got one shot at this, but they are the most talented group of players English rugby has ever had.'

Assistant coach Phil Larder, who had become an increasingly important figure in terms of England's tactics, explained why he felt the team was so strong. 'People in sport call it the "X factor",' said Larder, a former Great Britain rugby league coach. 'The Australian rugby league team have it. You see them as they arrive for a match. Not only do they know how to win, they expect to win. You can sense the same thing in the Australian cricket team and there was a hint of it in the great Wigan rugby league team of the 1990s. Manchester United in their element have it, as did the Leicester Tigers. It is always decisive in winning big matches.'

On the Wednesday before the final several important announcements were made. First came the news that André Watson would make history by becoming the first man to officiate at two World Cup finals. The forty-five-year-old South African, who was in charge when Australia beat France in the 1999 final, renowned for keeping matches flowing, and received the nod ahead of all the other neutral referees who had officiated at the tournament.

Then, Eddie Jones announced the Wallaby team from their Coff's Harbour base on the New South Wales coast. The only change from the team that had so comprehensively beaten the All Blacks in the semi-final was an enforced one. Al Baxter, in his first international season, was to complete a dream of a World Cup at tight head by coming in to replace the unfortunate Ben Darwin. The harrowing scenes of Darwin laying motionless on the turf against New Zealand were at least partly forgotten when the news emerged that he was not going to suffer any long-term after-effects from the injury to his neck. Among the many who had sent goodwill messages to him was Phil Vickery, one of the trio who would have been up against him in the front row in the final, had Darwin not suffered the injury.

Finally, Woodward announced his starting fifteen, plus England's seven substitutes, all of whom could be crucial. The one change to the starting line-up had been widely predicted: Mike Tindall, with his greater physical presence, returned in place of Mike Catt, who was dropped to the bench. There were two main reasons for this selection. First, England knew they had to dull the cutting edge of Wallaby centre Stirling Mortlock, who had sliced through the All Blacks' defence the week before. Second, it signalled a desire in the England camp to move the ball through the hands, rather than relying on the dual kicking strategy of Wilkinson and Catt. On the substitutes' bench was a selection of players who could have expected to walk into almost any other international starting fifteen. Alongside Catt were Lewis Moody, Dorian West, Kyran Bracken, Iain Balshaw and Martin Corry. Also there, as ever, was the most capped international of them all: Jason Leonard, hoping to receive his 113th cap on Saturday.

'It was right to go back to Tindall for this game,' Woodward explained. 'We are here to win this match. It's as simple as that. Sport can be a brutal business. You are either in the team or you are not. It's not easy. Tindall is a major part of our team and has been for some time. He fully understood why I made the change last week and now Mike Catt has also been brilliant in his attitude. He agrees that this is the best way to go into this match. I get paid to win test matches, after all.'

There were no fears of any resentment between the two Bath players, of course. The England management had already noticed how Tindall had saved his warmest embrace and strongest words of encouragement before the semi-final against France for Catt. 'I did it because I wanted them to win the game,' Tindall explained, after being told of his recall. 'These are all my best friends and my disappointment didn't make a blind bit of difference to that. You don't want to show your disappointment. You can't really, because you've got to be upbeat for everyone else so that you don't let any negativity creep into the team. Of course, I feel for Catty. He's done nothing wrong and it's hard to take. I know, because I was in his position the previous week. I was the first to pat him on the back last week and he was the first to do the same to me once the team was read out.'

Catt, displaying again the relaxed attitude he's shown of late, was able to joke about his omission. 'I'll let Tins get beaten up for sixty minutes, then I'll come on and produce the goods,' he said. 'I'm just glad to be part of the squad. Being part of a World Cup final in any shape or form is great, especially as I got in at the eleventh hour. I had an inkling this might happen. Australia play a different way to France.'

As for the rest of the squad, many were eager to express their hopes and desires in this, the most important week of their lives. Lawrence Dallaglio, openly weeping during the national anthem before the semi-final kicked-off, said, 'Yes, there were tears, but you have to understand just how important that semi-final was to the whole team. The intervening four years since the disappointment of the last World Cup have been tough, both physically and mentally. The whole squad has a shared commitment and we rely on each other, but to hear so many thousands of England fans belting out the anthem was fantastic. I am sure we will get just as much backing in the final, even though we are playing the host nation.

We've been telling everyone who cares to listen that we haven't come here to finish second. Australia are a very good side, and they showed tremendous defensive qualities against New Zealand, but they scored only one try, and that was from an interception. They will be asked huge questions by an England team that has won the past four matches between the countries.'

> 'I'll let Tins get beaten up for sixty minutes, then I'll come on and produce the goods.'
>
> MIKE CATT *on losing his place to Bath team-mate Mike Tindall*

England's number eight continued, 'Many critics are looking at the two back rows and saying it's going to be a contest that could have a huge impact on the final result. But the back row can only operate if the front-five forwards are doing the business, and that was the case against France. Hilly, Backy and myself benefited from the work of the other five forwards.'

Jonny Wilkinson, meanwhile, revealed that his new friend, David Beckham, had been in touch again. 'He wished me luck, which is great coming from him, because he's the best at what he does,' said Wilkinson, one of the few sportsmen who could now rival England's football captain in iconic status back home. 'He is very supportive, and chatting to him allows me to catch up with what's going on elsewhere and think about something else for a while.

'Generally, none of us are thinking at this stage of anything else [but the match], and certainly not the final whistle and what goes on after that,' he added. 'All we want to do is be properly prepared so that we can cope with whatever comes our way. All I want to be afterwards is proud of the way I went about it.'

Back home in England for the international match against Denmark, Beckham reiterated his support for the whole team. 'I'd love to be out in Australia,' he said. 'I'm not a great rugby man, but since I've become friends with

Jonny, I've become much more interested in it. To watch what they are doing and the way they are performing, especially the way the national anthem was sung the other day, is pretty amazing. If they go all the way and win it, then, hopefully, we can do as well one day. I'm sure we're going to win. It will be a tight game and a hard match, but the way England are playing and the passion they are showing, with the country behind them, they've got a great chance. They went over there with a great deal of expectation, but the way Jonny and the rest of the squad have performed has been a credit to the nation.'

'It will be a tight game and a hard match, but the way England are playing and the passion they are showing, with the country behind them, they've got a great chance.'

DAVID BECKHAM

In Sydney, Will Greenwood dwelled for a moment on past Anglo-Aussie battles. 'As a kid, you grew up marvelling at the Ashes, the Kangaroos and the rest, and we always seem to come out on the wrong side of the ledger,' said the centre. 'But my brother sent me a text message – "Remember Ian Botham in 1981" – so we've had our moments. As players, you think of Daley Thompson in 1980, the Ashes a year later, and we would love to have Sydney 2003 etched into the history books. But I'm sure there's an Australian fifteen who will have something to say about that.'

Josh Lewsey was happy to talk of what playing in the final meant to him. 'It's a massive privilege,' said the full-back. 'Although we effectively just chase a pig's bladder around the field for a living, we have the ability to touch so many. The other day we were introduced to a guy who was terminally ill with cancer and his last wish was to come and watch England in the World Cup. Things like that put everything into perspective.'

Lewsey was quick not to read too much into England's win in June in Melbourne. 'They were missing a lot of players then,' he insisted. 'They're back to full strength now, though, and their confidence is high. We'll have to perform a lot better than we did then to win again. We'll have to play heads-up rugby to the best of our ability.'

Win or lose, Lewsey's first action after the final will be to text the result to an army friend serving in Iraq. He knew he could well have

'My brother sent me a text message – "Remember Ian Botham in 1981".'

WILL GREENWOOD

been there himself if his life had taken a different course and he'd chosen to remain in the services, rather than playing rugby professionally. 'I got a message from one of my army friends on duty somewhere in the middle of Iraq,' he revealed. 'He said they hadn't been able to see last week's semi-final and they wouldn't be able to see the final, either. He asked me to let him know how we got on as soon as I can after the match, and that, hopefully, will give them all a morale boost. I'll text him the score as soon as I get back to the dressing room. If it gives him a lift, fantastic. When my former col-leagues now in Iraq tell me some of the stories from out there, it again puts what I do for a living into some perspective. How can I compare the pressure I'm under with the pressure they're facing? I don't have to dig a trench, turn up at a bombed building and pick up dismembered bodies. What they are doing is real life, whereas what I'll be doing is playing in a game, albeit a very important game.'

If Lewsey was keeping things in perspective, his captain was keeping everyone focused. 'With him, there's no way anyone's going to get carried away and not be totally ready for Saturday,' explained assistant coach Andy Robinson. 'He has the skill of getting his message across in the fewest possi-ble words. There's no bullshit. He's learned that from various coaches over the years. He chooses the right words. They're never flash, but he always seems to capture the right moment. His timing is always spot on. As for the final itself, Johnno never goes on to a pitch feeling he deserves anything. He doesn't want anything given to him. He will go out there and earn that medal.'

> '**He doesn't want anything given to him. He will go out there and earn that medal.**'
>
> ANDY ROBINSON on Martin Johnson

Alongside Martin Johnson in the scrum, as he had been throughout England's rise to the top of the world rankings, would be club col-league Ben Kay. The six-foot-six lock was looking to extend his run of seven consecutive wins over Southern Hemisphere opposition on Saturday, and, more than anyone, he appreci-ated the qualities Johnson brought to the England team. 'You'd always want Johnno on your side,' he said. 'He performs consistently week in, week out, as though every game is the most important one of his life. That's one of his big strengths. Another is that he's very honest. You'll never see Johnno trying to impress anyone, but you'll always see him getting on with his job. As a captain, he has the knack of knowing when enough has been said. He has got used to the role and made it his own. One of the most telling things he said to me was after his daughter Molly had been born. He said: "I can go home after losing a game and she doesn't care whether we have won or lost." That's a good way of keeping it all in perspective.'

Kay voiced the feelings of the whole team when he underlined the pressure England, the favourites, were under, not least from themselves. 'The memory of winning will stay with us for ever, but so too would the memory of losing,' he confessed. 'This would seem to be the best chance we have of ever winning the World Cup. Our motivation before the semi-final was that the last thing we wanted was to have to go into a third–fourth-place play-off game. The motivation this week is that we don't want to be making a twenty-four-hour flight home with boxes of tissues in our hands. Players and management have sacrificed a lot in the past few years. It would be a shame to have gone through all that and not to have a winner's medal to show for it. We have been given this opportunity and now it's up to us to take it.'

> **'The motivation this week is that we don't want to be making a twenty-four-hour flight home with boxes of tissues in our hands.'**
>
> *BEN KAY*

Jason Leonard – on the bench, but destined to get his usual run-out, although not in regulation time – was the sole member of the side who could personally avenge the defeat of twelve years earlier. 'It's been a long old wait to get a second bite of the cherry, hasn't it?' the prop mused. 'To be honest, I never imagined it would come again. I've been very lucky to have been involved in four World Cup campaigns, all of which have been enjoyable, with many highs, and obviously one or two lows as well. But this current team seems able to come up with all the answers. We can play the game any way you like. Let's just hope we come up with the right answer on Saturday night.'

Scrum-half Matt Dawson, who had won the keenly contested battle for the number-nine shirt ahead of sub Kyran Bracken and the unlucky Andy Gomarsall, talked of how his dream of winning the World Cup had developed over the years. 'I can't say I always dreamed of playing in a World Cup final as a schoolboy or mini-rugby player, because the World Cup only started in 1987,' he explained. 'I never ran around the school playground scoring tries in the World Cup Final. But I first really started taking notice of the World Cup in 1995, when I missed out on selection for Jack Rowell's squad. I loved what I saw from South Africa and made a vow then that not only would I play in a World Cup final, but we would be winners. That is still my dream and now we have the chance of making it reality.'

The Australians, of course, had dreams of their own. Happily, in the week when it would matter most, coach Eddie Jones spoke positively of both the opposition and, indeed, of his opposite number. 'Clive has taken a side who were very conservative and has turned them into a side who can play any

The English national anthem, prior to the kick-off the Final in the Telstra Stadium, Sydney, 22nd November 2003 (*Mark Dadswell/Getty Images*).

Matt Dawson releases the ball (*Nick Laham/Getty Images*).

Mike Tindall powers through the Australian lines (*Nick Laham/Getty Images*).

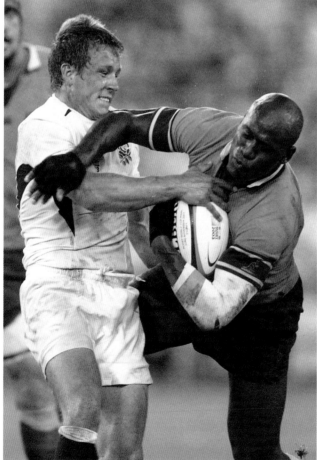

He doesn't just kick the ball; Jonny Wilkinson's tackling was first-class during the Final (*Adam Pretty/Getty Images*).

Jason Robinson dives for the corner: the crucial try on 38 minutes that put England 14-5 ahead (*both Nick Laham/Getty Images*).

Above and right: That drop goal; Jonny Wilkinson (and, opposite top) a second after the ball sails through the posts (*Stuart Hannagan/ David Rogers/Nick Laham/ Getty Images*).

Martin Johnson on the final whistle (*Chris McGrath/Getty Images*).

The ecstasy: Lawrence Dallaglio, Will Greenwood, the players and the management team celebrate . . . (*Adam Pretty/Stuart Hannagan/ Nick Laham/Mark Nolan/Daniel Berehulak/Getty Images*).

The world's greatest no.10; and the England coach with the trophy (*Daniel Berehulak/Jon Buckle/Nick Laham/Getty Images*).

number of ways: with width, or kicking, or defensively,' Jones said. 'We saw this in June when they were widely criticised for playing the kicking game against New Zealand in the rain, but then they came to Melbourne and played forty minutes against Australia which was probably the best ball movement we've seen this year. That's a great achievement. England have beaten us the last four times and that may give them a psychological advantage, but we have only six of the guys who started that match in June. It's a different Australian team, a different attitude, a different style of play, different strengths and weaknesses. Our game is about as developed as it can get. We are ready to give it a really good go.'

On the subject of Jonny Wilkinson, Jones made one of the few sensible points to emerge from the host nation all week. Elsewhere, a newspaper had offered a voodoo doll of the England fly-half for pin-sticking, and the general consensus Down Under was that if Wilkinson could be stopped, so could England. Jones astutely observed that it was not as simple as that. 'We have probably spoken about Jonny less than any other player,' he said. 'Certainly we respect him as a player, but for us it's important he isn't blown out of all proportion. It's going to depend on the forward contest. You can't get to any fly-half if your pack is not going forward.'

For his part, Clive Woodward was ready for any eventuality in the match. 'When the guys run out on to the pitch on Saturday night, we like to feel we know how the game will unfold, but if it doesn't, we'll have to change things through the eighty minutes,' he said. 'You go in with a game-plan, believing you know what is going to work, but if the opposition do something totally differently, you can't just accept that you've been caught out. You have to adapt immediately at the next scrum or line-out and just do it. We're expecting the Wallabies to come at us at one hundred miles an hour from the first kick off until, probably, the last. It couldn't be any other way, could it?

'They think that they have the edge by the way they play, the fitness of their team and their ability to attack wide. All I can say is that there is nothing I would change going into this game, absolutely nothing, in terms of training or selection. It gives you a certain amount of inner confidence. We'll be ready. To be honest, I'm still pinching myself because we are going into a World Cup final with the strongest possible team, with everyone fit

'I'm still pinching myself because we are going into a World Cup final with the strongest possible team, with everyone fit and everyone raring to go. That's why there is a quiet confidence about the team.'

CLIVE WOODWARD

and everyone raring to go. That's why there is a quiet confidence about the team. They want to get the job done.

'Whatever happens, win or lose, we have thrown everything into this. That's why I passionately believe that if England start well, we can win this game. The adrenaline will be pumping like it never has pumped before, so we have to keep our feet firmly on the ground and try to treat it like any other game. It's still fifteen men against fifteen. I don't care how we win the game, as long as we do. But I am convinced England's best performance in this whole tournament will come on Saturday night. We can win the World Cup.'

The final words before the biggest game in the history of rugby union, played out in front of the largest crowd and the biggest television audience, and probably the most important day in British sport since the summer of 1966, fell to the two captains. For George Gregan, this World Cup campaign had been a triumph already. Despite being on the receiving end of heavy criticism, he had steered his unfancied Wallabies to the final, and now he was speaking with a great deal of sense and maturity. 'We're going to need discipline in everything we do,' he said. 'In attack and defence. That will go a long way towards finding our way on the field.' His next comment revealed a level pragmatism of which Martin Johnson would have been proud. 'I don't believe in destiny,' said Gregan. 'I believe in reality. I also believe in hard work and planning. Then fate, destiny, whatever you want to call it, falls into your hands. It would mean everything to win the World Cup. It would mean all the hard work and sacrifices had been worth it. You can't understand from the outside how big a role in our lives this has been.'

Johnson echoed these sentiments. 'We've won nothing yet,' he was keen to remind his team. 'We've not achieved our goal yet. We had one, single aim and we've had it ever since we lost in the quarter-final four years ago. That defeat has haunted me ever since. Not just the fact that we lost, but *how* we lost, by five drop goals to which we had no answer. So now it's only ever been about winning the World Cup. To go home as losing finalists is not what it's all about, and never has been. It should be an incredible occasion, an incredible game, and I have complete respect for the Wallabies. It will be tight, will probably be decided only in the final quarter, maybe even in the last ten minutes. But we're as ready as we can be. We're going to give it our all, every single one of us, and I'm hoping – and expecting – this to be enough. We know we can beat Australia, but we also know we'll have to be at our best.'

And so the stage was set. Since 1966 the English sporting cupboard had been largely bare, often because of the superiority of a certain Antipodean nation. Even in the very week before the rugby union World Cup Final, the Australians had reasserted their dominance in the other code, winning yet another tight rugby league test series. Now England had the chance to redress the balance.

The host nation had tried all week to drum up support for their team. Australians were urged to go about their business wearing the Wallaby shirt. The Opera House was bathed in gold light to remind the thousands of English fans in Sydney that they were in hostile territory, even when they were sightseeing. Back in England, a wet and windy Saturday dawned with bars and rugby clubs throughout the land throwing open their doors and soon becoming packed to the rafters.

But if it was typically rainy in England, Sydney was in the grip of a virtual monsoon. The two teams had awoken to leaden skies, thick, low cloud and sporadic downpours. Everyone – the English gleefully; the Australians mournfully – asserted that the weather played into England's hands. They were, after all, the team that liked to keep it tight, the team that relied on a metronomic kicking machine, while the Australians were all flair and dash, which would inevitably be blunted by the conditions. That was the theory, anyway. Come Saturday night in Sydney, anyone who'd made a prediction that they knew exactly how this game would go must have been eating their words.

By the evening, the torrential rain had eased to drizzle, and both teams were confident that they would be able to parade their skills on rugby union's biggest stage. Occasionally, they did indeed dazzle; at other times they floundered. But what the forty players who ultimately took the field on Saturday, 22 November 2003 did provide was just about the most extraordinary game of rugby ever witnessed. No playwright would have had the nerve to write a script like the one that unfolded that night: it was simply too fantastic to be believed. Especially if you were English.

The dramatic sequence of events was made even more absorbing, of course, because this was the sport's showpiece, the World Cup Final. This match would have lived long in the memory if it had been nothing more than a club game, but as Jonny Wilkinson watched his drop goal sail between the posts, he surely must have known that he'd carved himself permanently into English sporting folklore alongside Geoff Hurst and Ian Botham. That last-minute kick allowed him to join an elite group who can say that they lifted the mood of a nation. And last minute is not even doing this justice. Twenty seconds would be nearer the mark. Just twenty seconds from the end of extra time – with rugby's first ever period of sudden-death 'extra-extra time' looming, and maybe even a drop-goal shoot-out after that – Wilkinson let fly with his supposedly unfavoured right boot to send half of those in the Telstra Stadium into ecstasy. And a couple of bounces off a satellite later, the pubs, clubs and living rooms of England followed suit.

The key figures in the move were fitting. Captain Martin Johnson, at the end of his finest performance in a white shirt, drove his huge frame into the Wallaby pack, creating time and space behind him. Scrum-half Matt Dawson, who seconds earlier had raced up the field to reduce the distance to the posts by a good ten metres, spun the ball back. And Wilkinson struck. It was not the fly-half's best strike by any means. It was certainly not pretty. But who cared? Nobody in England, that's for sure.

There was barely time for the shell-shocked Wallabies to kick off again. From the restart, Mike Catt, who had made his mark since coming on for the injured Mike Tindall, hoofed the ball high and far into the stands and referee André Watson blew his whistle. Johnson raised both arms and looked up to the heavens. Neil Back raced to the stands, plucked his four-year-old daughter from the crowd, and went on to collect his winner's medal with little Olivia still in his arms. Wilkinson smiled and waved at the sea of white jerseys that filled the end where his drop goal had won the World Cup for England. And everybody danced.

The last time there had been anything to rival this had been nearly four decades earlier. And England's victory had many strange echoes from that glorious day in 1966. Most uncanny of all was that one family provided a member of both teams. Ben Cohen, of course, became the second member of his family to pick up a World Cup winner's medal, after his uncle George had played at right-back against West Germany. Then there were the weird similarities in the games themselves. On both occasions England had seemed in control, had heard their fans celebrating in the stands, only for a never-say-die opposition to equalise with the last kick of the game in regulation time. Then England had regrouped, motivated by an inspirational captain, imposed themselves in extra time, and created the opportunity for their number ten to write himself into the history books with a thumping kick in the dying seconds. So, hardly surprisingly, within seconds of the final whistle, comparisons were being drawn between Martin Johnson and Bobby Moore, between Jonny Wilkinson and Geoff Hurst, and between Sir Alf Ramsey and (Sir?) Clive Woodward.

Again rather like the 1966 football World Cup Final, early on there was little to suggest the drama to come. That was because England, after a shaky start, were so dominant. But that shaky start had been disconcerting. Australia took the lead after just six minutes. Having refused two potentially kickable penalties in order to retain possession and go for the try, the ball was eventually passed to Stephen Larkham. The visionary stand-off then sent a clever cross-field punt towards the left wing, and stood back to watch the ensuing contest between two of the most successful recruits to the union code from rugby league. Jason Robinson rarely loses out to anyone, but this was a serious mismatch. Lote Tuqiri, enjoying a massive height advantage, plucked the ball from high above Robinson's head to touch down in the corner. Flatley missed the conversion, but the Wallabies were still 0–5 up.

As England had already proved against Samoa, Wales and France in this tournament, though, they can deal with early setbacks. Five minutes later Wilkinson converted his first penalty of the evening after the Wallabies were penalised for not staying on their feet in the maul. Another eight minutes went by and England had nudged ahead through a second Wilkinson penalty. The stand-off thereby became the tournament's leading points scorer, overtaking France's Frédéric Michalak. (Wilkinson would eventually finish with 113 points, 10 clear of his nearest rival.)

The game seemed to have found its level, and you could almost hear the Australian scribes sharpening their pencils to describe how their gallant, adventurous side were defeated by England's kicking robot. But that would have been a gross distortion of what was happening on the pitch. With the ball slippery, there were the expected handling errors, but England, just as much as the Australians, were prepared to run the ball when the opportunity presented itself. And they were doing so with greater success, too, even though they hadn't as yet managed to cross the Wallaby line.

But they soon came close; *really* close. Unfortunately, on the wing to run in a simple chance after a flowing move was not Cohen, Lewsey or Robinson, but Ben Kay. A massive tackle by Wilkinson on replacement Australian stand-off Matt Giteau resulted in a turnover and a three-on-one overlap for England to exploit. Lewsey passed to Dawson, Dawson passed to Kay, and all the big lock forward had to do was catch the ball and fall over the line. Instead, he dropped the ball and knocked on. The agony on his face was clear for all to see. If England had not ultimately won the match, he would have been haunted by what had just happened for the rest of his days.

Kay's nerves must have been calmed somewhat when a third Wilkinson penalty went over in the 28th minute. The stand-off hadn't been immaculate up to that point (he'd snatched at a drop goal just before putting in that big hit on Giteau), but his place-kicking had been superb in what were still testing conditions. England were 9–5 up, and within ten minutes they'd drawn comfortably clear.

Lawrence Dallaglio made a thrilling break before flicking a cute inside pass to Wilkinson. With a couple of options, Wilkinson certainly chose the right one by passing to Jason Robinson on the wing. Almost anyone else would still have had a fair bit to do, but Robinson simply turned on the afterburners and ran past the Australian defence, who didn't lay a finger on him as he gleefully slid over the line. Robinson punched the ball, Aussie Rules style, into the crowd in delight. Although Wilkinson missed the conversion, it seemed to all the world that the game was over. The half-time whistle blew with England 14–5 ahead, and the English players cantered purposefully off the field and back to what must have been a very content dressing room.

For Australia to have any chance of staging a comeback, they had to score first after the break. And they did. In the first of a series of errors that plagued England in the second half, they were caught offside and Elton Flatley made his first successful kick of the night. All of a sudden, the tide of the game seemed to have turned: England were on the back foot and the Wallabies surged forward. Flatley missed with his next penalty chance – the decision to kick for goal from a potentially try-scoring position having been greeted with derisive jeers by the English fans in the crowd – but he made amends on 61 minutes after Phil Vickery was caught with his hands in the ruck. Now England were consistently infringing, at least according to Referee Watson. But when the South African penalised England's seemingly dominant scrum three times in a row, there was genuine confusion among *all* the players, not just the English.

However, in spite of the Australian fightback and the idiosyncratic refereeing, it seemed that England would cling on. They hadn't managed to score in the second half, with Wilkinson missing another drop goal in the 72nd minute, but time was almost up. Then the English scrum was penalised yet again, and Flatley had a tricky kick to tie the scores. To his enormous credit, the Wallaby centre converted what must be one of the all-time pressure kicks to drag this thriller into extra time. There was not even any time for a restart. Up in the management's box Clive Woodward slammed his fist down on a desk in frustration. The momentum was now obviously with the Wallabies.

Or at least it should have been. Clearly failing to understand the concept of defeat, Wilkinson knocked over a mammoth, fifty-metre penalty a minute into the first period of extra time. It cleared the bar by a matter of inches, and should have quelled the Australian fire. It did not. They fought for all they were worth, but over the next eighteen minutes could not find a way through. However, crucially, they had not fallen further behind, as first Catt and then Wilkinson (for the third time) erred with drop-goal efforts. But England were giving the Wallabies nothing, having cut out the infringements. Until, that is, the second last gasp of the night was upon us. In the penultimate minute, Dallaglio was adjudged to have handled in the ruck, and Flatley again had the weight of a nation on his shoulders. As unflappable as ever, he slotted over the kick. There was one difference between now and earlier, though. There was just enough time for a restart.

Martin Johnson takes up the story. 'We knew that if we kicked long at the restart we should be able to force Australia to kick for touch to give us a line-out,' he explained. 'I'd be lying if I said the drop goal was planned, though. We were just attacking and hoping. I took the ball into the ruck and was on the floor when Jonny struck the drop goal. I just managed to look up and see the ball sail through the posts. Even then I didn't think the game was won. I knew that if Australia kept possession from their restart, they might be able to set up a drop goal for themselves, or even get a penalty awarded. When I saw Mike Catt with the ball I screamed at him just to kick it anywhere, but make sure the ball went out.'

Catt duly obliged, Referee Watson made sweet music with his whistle, and England erupted. Minutes later, Johnson was collecting the William Webb Ellis Trophy from an ashen-faced Australian Prime Minister, John Howard, before leading his men on a lap of honour around the Telstra Stadium.

England had just become the first Northern Hemisphere nation to win the World Cup after sixteen years of Southern Hemisphere dominance. In doing so they had notched up an unprecedented fifth straight win over Australia. Jonny Wilkinson had now dropped more goals, eight, than anyone in the history of the Rugby World Cup. Jason Leonard had won his world record-stretching 113th cap by coming on late to replace Phil Vickery. He now also had a winner's medal to add the runners-up medal he'd earned in 1991. Australia's loss meant that no world champions had yet been able to defend their title. This was the third consecutive final in which the team who scored first had gone on to lose. And Australia now joined England in having lost a final on home soil.

But far more important than the statistics were the post-match emotions. The hero of the hour, Jonny Wilkinson, could finally smile. 'I didn't want the game to go to a drop-goal competition,' he explained. 'I just wanted to win so much for the other guys. I had to make sure I hit the target when the chance came my way. Now I've got no voice left. It's what we've fought so long for. I want to hold on to this moment for as long as possible. It was a long old game, wasn't it? In my dreams last night it wasn't that long. It's one of those nights I'll never forget: the night we won the World Cup.'

Neil Back talked of his spontaneous decision to find his family. 'Having a visual-awareness coach with England recently has paid dividends,' he joked. 'I spotted them immediately in the crowd. I would have taken my son, but he's only a year old and wanted to cling to his mother.' In a reference to the

> 'Even then I didn't think the game was won ... When I saw Mike Catt with the ball I screamed at him just to kick it anywhere, but make sure the ball went out.'
>
> *MARTIN JOHNSON*
> *on the last seconds of the match*

> 'I just wanted to win so much for the other guys. I had to make sure I hit the target when the chance came my way.'
>
> *JONNY WILKINSON*

slating he and his back-row colleagues had put up with from the Australian press, Back continued, 'So much for Dad's Army, eh? We've learned how to win. At no point in that game did I think we were going to lose. In fact, I've been confident all year we'd win the World Cup.'

A beaming Phil Vickery was particularly emotional. 'My mum's just told me that people can say what they like about me, but from now on I am a World Cup-winner and I will have that winner's medal for the rest of my life. Words escape me. It's a great day for English rugby, and it's a great day for England. It's what dreams are made of.'

> **'So much for Dad's Army, eh?'**
> *NEIL BACK*

Ben Cohen was still pinching himself an hour after the game. 'I'm lost for words,' he declared. 'It's unbelievable. Incredible. It's been a carbon copy of 1966, hasn't it? What with the late equaliser from the opposition, and then England hitting the winner. Just think, the two greatest moments in English sport, thirty-seven years apart, and the Cohen family's been involved in both.' With that, the England winger went off to celebrate with his uncle George.

Will Greenwood said, 'We told ourselves before the game that we would leave nothing out there when we came off the pitch. Our aim was to come off the field as spent men. At the end I didn't know what to do. Jump? Sing? Laugh? Cry? I just feel so very privileged to be a part of this amazing team.

> **'Our aim was to come off the field as spent men. At the end I didn't know what to do. Jump? Sing? Laugh? Cry? I just feel so very privileged to be part of this amazing team.'**
> *WILL GREENWOOD*

'As for Jonny Wilkinson, what can you say about the kid? He's so special. He's a fantastic talent. That's why, when Wilko received his medal on the podium, all the rest of the England squad stood and applauded. I've never seen him miss four drop-goal attempts in a match, so the law of averages suggested he'd get it right. He just happened to choose the most dramatic moment possible to deliver.'

'It's all very surreal,' admitted Matt Dawson. 'It's been a long four years since we lost in the quarter-final of the World Cup, but all the work, all the sacrifices and all the setbacks along the way have been worth it. Well worth it.' His Northampton team-mate Steve Thompson added: 'I just can't believe we're going to be taking the World Cup back home with us. If it really is just a dream, then make sure I never wake up.' Lawrence Dallaglio insisted he

'As for Jonny Wilkinson, what can you say about the kid? He's so special. He's a fantastic talent … I've never seen him miss four drop-goal attempts in a match, so the law of averages suggests he'd get it right.'

WILL GREENWOOD

would make the most of the moment: 'You've got to savour it, haven't you?' he reasoned.

The Australians were magnanimous in defeat. 'Two world-class teams going at it hammer and tongs,' reflected their captain George Gregan. 'Congratulations must be extended to England. They delivered under pressure, and they delivered when it counted. Jonny Wilkinson is outstanding under pressure. He missed a few early in the match but he knocked over the one that counted and you've got to take your hat off to him for that.'

Coach Eddie Jones, too, earned many friends that night. 'The better team won,' he conceded. 'There's no doubt about that. England deserve their moment because of the work they've put in, the coaching and the character of the players.'

His counterpart, Clive Woodward, was understandably overjoyed. 'I feel ecstatic for every single person with a white shirt at the ground,' he said. 'It makes you so proud to be English. It means that I have a medal round my neck and a gold cup in the cupboard. I'd like to thank the supporters, who were just fantastic. Our Dad's Army came through, didn't they? Jonny dropped the winning goal. So all those comments made about our pack and Jonny by the opposition will now come back to haunt them. The memories from tonight will live for ever.'

The last word on this momentous achievement, however, must fall to England's inspirational captain. Sporting deification would be bestowed on Martin Johnson when he returned home two days later, but immediately after the game he was simply relieved and happy that the long journey had come to a successful conclusion. 'It's going to take days, maybe even weeks, to sink in,' he admitted. 'It's been a long, long campaign. And it's been hard, so very hard. The pool game against South Africa put more pressure on us than at any other time I can remember. We struggled against Samoa. We struggled against Wales, too. But after the Welsh game I started dreaming of this moment. That's when I realised we really could win the World Cup, and that I might just be collecting the trophy. If we'd lost the final after having such a lead, I'm not sure that I ever would have properly recovered from it.

'The better team won … England deserve their moment because of the work they've put in, the coaching and the character of the players.'

EDDIE JONES

We knew we were the better team, but we almost blew it. Thankfully, we just about held our nerve, and that man Wilkinson did it again for us, didn't he? He must have the best scriptwriter in the business working for him, but we're so very glad he's part of our team. And I'm so very glad we've finally won the World Cup.'

As is the whole of England, probably the whole of Britain, and maybe even the whole of the Northern Hemisphere. It was an incredible World Cup tournament, an amazing World Cup Final, and the most dramatic conclusion to any sporting event for years.

And now, and for at least the next four years, England could call themselves world champions.

'Sounds good, doesn't it?' said Martin Johnson as he headed off into the Sydney night.

Indeed it does.

TOURNAMENT RESULTS

A

Ireland
Australia
Argentina
Romania
Namibia

Australia 24–8 Argentina
Ireland 45–17 Romania
Argentina 67 –14 Namibia
Australia 90–8 Romania
Ireland 64–7 Namibia
Argentina 50–3 Romania
Australia 142–0 Namibia
Argentina 15–16 Ireland
Namibia 7–37 Romania
Ireland 16–17 Australia

AUSTRALIA = *Winners*
Ireland = *Runners up*

B

France
Fiji
Scotland
USA
Japan

France 61–18 Fiji
Scotland 32–11 Japan
Fiji 19 –18 USA
France 51–29 Japan
Scotland 39–15 USA
Fiji 41–13 Japan
France 51–9 Scotland
Japan 26–39 USA
France 41–14 USA
Scotland 22–20 Fiji

FRANCE = *Winners*
Scotland = *Runners up*

C

England
South Africa
Samoa
Uruguay
Georgia

South Africa 72–6 Uruguay
England 84–6 Georgia
Samoa 60 –13 Uruguay
South Africa 6–25 England
Georgia 9–46 Samoa
South Africa 46–19 Georgia
England 35–22 Samoa
Georgia 12–24 Uruguay
South Africa 60–10 Samoa
England 111–13 Uruguay

ENGLAND = *Winners*
South Africa = *Runners up*

D

New Zealand
Wales
Italy
Canada
Tonga

New Zealand 70–7 Italy
Wales 41–10 Canada
Italy 36 –12 Tonga
New Zealand 68–6 Canada
Wales 27–20 Tonga
Italy 19–14 Canada
New Zealand 91–7 Tonga
Italy 15–27 Wales
Canada 24–7 Tonga
New Zealand 53–37 Wales

NEW ZEALAND = *Winners*
Wales = *Runners up*

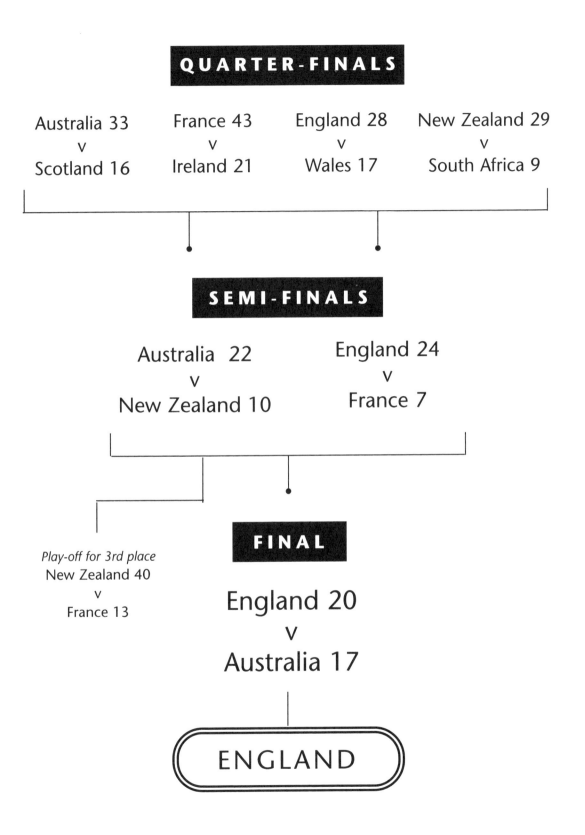

QUARTER-FINALS

Australia 33
v
Scotland 16

France 43
v
Ireland 21

England 28
v
Wales 17

New Zealand 29
v
South Africa 9

SEMI-FINALS

Australia 22
v
New Zealand 10

England 24
v
France 7

Play-off for 3rd place
New Zealand 40
v
France 13

FINAL

England 20
v
Australia 17

ENGLAND

Tony Biscombe,
Video Analyst

Richard Prescott,
Director of
Communications

Phil Keith-Roach,
Assistant Coach

Barney Kenny,
Physio

Dave Reddin,
Fitness Coach

Simon Hardy
Assistant Coach

Phil Pask,
Physio

Dave Campbell,
Chef

Louise Ramsay,
Manager

Sherylle Calder, Visual
Awareness Coach

Simon Kemp,
Doctor

Richard Wegrzyk,
Masseur

Steve Lander,
RFU Referee

Dave Alred,
Assistant Coach

Andy Robinson,
Coach

Richard Smith,
Legal Adviser

Dave Tennison,
Kitman

Phil Larder,
Assistant Coach

Rugby World Cup England Management Team 2003